Computing

Roger Legg

Contents

Chapter 1   Applications of computers

Chapter 2   Computer hardware

Chapter 3   Data representation

Chapter 4   System software

Specification lists

AQA Computing

MODULE	SPECIFICATION TOPIC	CHAPTER REFERENCE	STUDIED IN CLASS	REVISED	PRACTICE QUESTIONS
Module 1 (M1)	Fundamentals of computer systems	1.2, 2.1, 2.2			
	Fundamentals of programming	4.1, 4.2, 4.3, 8.1, 8.2, 8.3, 8.4			
	Fundamentals of information and data representation	3.1, 3.2, , 6.1, 6.2			
	Communication and networking	5.1, 5.2			
Module 2 (M2)	Applications and effects	1.1, 1.2, 1.3			
	Files and databases	6.1, 6.2, 6.3, 6.4, 6.5			
	Operating systems	4.1			
	Hardware devices	2.2, 2.3			
Module 3 (M3)	Systems development	7.1, 7.2, 7.3			

Examination analysis

The specification comprises three compulsory modules.

Modules 1 and 2 will be assessed by written examinations that contain short-answer questions and longer structured questions. Module 3 will be assessed by a written examination containing structured questions based on a practical computing exercise. In each case all questions will be compulsory.

Module 1	written paper	1 hr 30 min	35%
Module 2	written paper	1 hr 30 min	35%
Module 3	written paper	1 hr 30 min	30%

OCR Computing

MODULE	SPECIFICATION TOPIC	CHAPTER REFERENCE	STUDIED IN CLASS	REVISED	PRACTICE QUESTIONS
Module 1 (M1)	Components of a computer system	2.1, 2.2, 2.3, 4.1			
	System software	4.1, 4.2, 4.3			
	Programming tools and techniques	4.3, 8.1, 8.3, 8.4			
	Data: its representation, structure and manipulation	3.1, 3.2, 6.1, 6.2, 6.5, 8.2			
	Hardware	2.1, 2.2, 2.3			
	Data transmission and networking	5.1, 5.2			
Module 2 (M2)	Design	7.2, 7.3			
	Testing	7.2			
	Implementation	7.2			
Module 3 (M3)	Systems development life cycle	7.1, 7.2, 7.3			
	Applications software	1.1, 1.2			
	Handling of data in information systems	2.2, 2.3, 6.2, 6.3, 6.4			
	User interface	7.3			
	Characteristics of information systems	6.3			
	Implications of computer use	1.1, 1.3			

Examination analysis

The specification comprises three compulsory modules.

Module 1 will be assessed by a written examination containing 10–15 structured questions. Module 3 will be assessed by a written examination containing 6–8 structured questions based on short scenarios. Module 2 will be assessed by 3–5 structured tasks that will ask the candidates to find solutions to given problems.

Module 1	written paper	1 hr 30 min	30%
Module 2	Coursework		40%
Module 3	written paper	1 hr 30 min	30%

Edexcel Computing

MODULES	SPECIFICATION TOPIC	CHAPTER REFERENCE	STUDIED IN CLASS	REVISED	PRACTICE QUESTIONS
Module 1 (<u>M1</u>)	Fundamentals of computer systems	1.1, 1.2, 1.3			
	The range and scope of computer applications	1.1, 5.1, 5.2			
	The social, legal, ethical and economic implications of the use of computers	1.3			
	Data representation and security	3.2, 6.1, 6.2, 6.5			
	Software packages	1.2			
	Hardware	2.1, 2.2, 2.3			
	Networks and communications	5.1, 5.2			
	Operating system facilities	4.1			
	People	1.3			
	Key features of information systems	6.1, 6.2, 6.3, 6.4, 7.2, 7.3			
Module 2 (<u>M2</u>)	Systems analysis and design	6.3, 6.4, 7.1, 7.2, 7.3			
	Data organisations and types	3.1, 3.2, 6.1, 6.2, 6.3, 6.4			
	Algorithms, software design and implementation	4.2, 4.3, 7.1, 7.2, 8.1, 8.2, 8.3, 8.4			
Module 3 (<u>M3</u>)	Systems analysis	7.1, 7.2			
	Systems design	7.1, 7.3			
	Systems specification prototyping	7.3			

Examination analysis

The specification comprises three compulsory modules.

Modules 1 and 2 will be assessed by written examination papers that consist of 4 or 5 short-answer questions and 2 longer structured questions. In each case all questions will be compulsory. Module 3 will be assessed by a project.

Module 1	written paper	1 hr 30 min	33.3%
Module 2	written paper	1 hr 30 min	33.3%
Module 3	Coursework		33.3%

WJEC Computing

MODULE	SPECIFICATION TOPIC	TOPIC REFERENCE	STUDIED IN CLASS	REVISED	PRACTICE QUESTIONS
Module CP 1	Systems analysis and design	6.3, 7.1, 7.2			
	Algorithms	8.4			
	Data types and data structures	3.2, 8.2			
	Sorting and searching	6.3			
	Program production	4.3, 8.1, 8.2, 8.3			
	Nature and type of software	1.1			
Module CP 2	Computer architecture	2.1			
	The operating system	4.1, 4.2, 4.3			
	Storage hierarchy	2.1, 2.2			
	Input/output peripheral equipment	2.3, 3.1, 3.2			
	Interfacing	2.1			
	Communication networks	5.1, 5.2			
	File organisation	6.2, 6,3			
	Software packages	1.2			
	Database systems	6.4			
	Data capture, verification and validation	2.3, 6.1			
	Typical computer applications and their associated hardware	1.1, 2.3, 5.2, 7.1, 7.2, 7.3			
	Consequences of current trends in the uses of computers	1.3			
	Privacy and security	1.3, 6.5			
Module CP 3	Analysis	7.1, 7.2			
	Design	7.1, 7.3			
	Planning	7.1, 7.2			
	Implementation	7.1, 7.2			
	Program documentation	7.3			
	Testing	7.2			
	Evaluation	7.1, 7.2			
	User documentation	7.1, 7.2, 7.3			

Examination analysis

The specification comprises three compulsory modules.

Modules CP 1 and CP 2 will be assessed by written examinations that consist of short-answer questions and longer structured questions. In each case all questions will be compulsory. Module CP 3 will be assessed by a project involving analysis, design and implementation, and documentation of a proposed solution.

Module CP 1	written paper	2 hr	33%
Module CP 2	written paper	2 hr	33%
Module CP 3	Coursework		34%

AS/A2 Level Computing courses

AS and A2

All Computing A Level courses being studied from September 2000 are in two parts, with three separate units or modules in each part. Most students will start by studying the AS (Advanced Subsidiary) course. Some will then go on to study the second part of the A Level course, called the A2. It is also possible to study the full A Level course, both AS and A2, in any order.

How will you be tested?

Assessment units

As well as being a choice of how the syllabuses are studied, there is also a choice of assessment. Of the three units that make up AS Computing, one contains some form of practical assessment. This may be a practical test set by the awarding body or it may be an assessment carried out by your teacher, based on the skills that you show on one or a number of practical tasks. Depending on the specification that you follow, part of a unit test may also be on an optional topic.

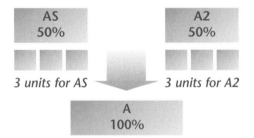

For AS Computing, you be tested by three assessment units. For the full A Level in Computing you will take a further three units. AS Computing forms 50% of the assessment weighting for the full A Level.

Each of these three tests can normally be taken in either January or June, so that you can take one or two tests part way through the course and leave the rest till the end or be assessed on the whole course when you have finished studying it. Any unit may be re-sat once.

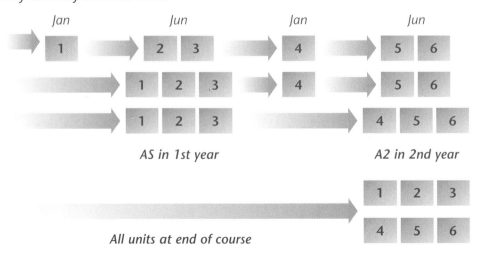

If you are disappointed with a module result, you can resit each module once. You will need to be very careful about when you take up a resit opportunity because you will have only one chance to improve your mark. The higher mark counts.

A2 and Synoptic assessment

For those students who, having studied AS, decide to go on to study A2, there are three further units to be studied. Similar assessment arrangements apply except some units, those that draw together various elements of the course in a 'synoptic' assessment, have to be assessed at the end of the course.

Coursework

Coursework will form part of your A Level Computing course. This will be in the form of a computing project that will assess your ability to design, test and implement a solution to a practical problem.

Key skills

It is important that you develop your key skills throughout the AS and A2 courses that you take, as these are skills that you need whatever you do beyond AS and A Levels. To gain the key skills qualification, which is equivalent to an AS Level, you will need to demonstrate that you have attained Level 3 in Communication, Application of number and Information technology. Part of the assessment can be done as normal class activity and part is by formal test.

It is a worthwhile qualification, as it demonstrates your ability to put your ideas across to other people, collect data and use up-to-date technology in your work.

What skills will I need?

Questions in A Level Computing examinations are designed to test a number of assessment objectives: these are skills and abilities that you should have acquired by studying the course. For the written papers at AS Level the main objectives being assessed are:

- recall of facts, terminology and relationships
- understanding of principles of operation of computer systems
- understanding of the application of computer systems
- explanation and interpretation of principles and concepts
- interpreting information given as numerical data or prose
- application of knowledge and understanding to familiar and unfamiliar situations.

Different types of questions in AS examinations

In AS Computing examinations, different types of questions are used to assess your abilities and skills.

These include short-answer questions, structured questions requiring both short answers and more extended answers, together with case studies to which you have to apply your knowledge. Multiple choice question papers are not used, although it is possible that some short-answer questions will use a multiple choice format, where you have to choose the correct response from a number of given alternatives.

Short-answer questions

A short-answer question may test recall or it may test understanding by requiring you to undertake a short calculation. Short-answer questions often have space for the answers printed on the question paper. Here is an example (the answer is shown in purple):

In the context of data stored on a magnetic tape, what is meant by **each** of the following:

(i) field
(ii) record
(iii) file?

(i) A numeric value or string of characters representing a single item of data
(ii) All the fields relating to one person or a single object (e.g. a stock item)
(iii) An organised collection of related records

Structured questions

Structured questions are in several parts. The parts are usually about a common context and they often become progressively more difficult and more demanding as you work your way through the question. They may start with simple recall, then test understanding of a familiar or an unfamiliar situation. The most difficult part of a structured question is usually at the end, where the candidate is sometimes asked to suggest a reason for a particular phenomenon or social implication.

When answering structured questions, do not feel that you have to complete one question before starting the next. The further you are into a question, the more difficult the marks are to obtain. If you run out of ideas, go on to the next question. Five minutes spent on the beginning of that question are likely to be much more fruitful than the same time spent wracking your brains trying to think of an explanation for an unfamiliar situation.

Here is an example of a structured question that becomes progressively more demanding.

(a) Draw a diagram showing how the microprocessor, data bus, address bus, control bus, memory and clock are interconnected in a computer system.

(b) Explain what hardware feature limits the amount of memory possible in a computer system.

(c) Describe **three** hardware design changes that would increase the speed of execution of programs.

Extended answers

In AS Level Computing, questions requiring more extended answers will usually form part of structured questions. They will normally appear at the end of structured questions and be characterised by having at least three marks (and often more) allocated to the answers as well as several lines (up to ten) of answer space. These questions are also used to assess your abilities to communicate ideas and put together a logical argument.

The 'correct' answers to extended questions are less well-defined than to those requiring short answers. Examiners may have a list of points for which credit is awarded up to the maximum for the question, or they may first of all judge the 'quality' of your response as poor, satisfactory or good before allocating it a mark within a range that corresponds to that 'quality'.

As an example of a question that requires an extended answer, a structured question on the use of storage devices could end with the following:

> Suggest why companies have chosen the CDROM as a suitable medium to distribute software and reference material. [8 marks]

Points that the examiners might look for include:

> The CD is read only so it is not going to be corrupted by users overwriting the information.
>
> The CD is extremely portable being light and fairly robust.
>
> It is not corrupted by magnetic fields so it does not have to be protected from them.
>
> It has a reasonable storage capacity, typically 640 Mbytes.
>
> The transfer speed is relatively slow but it is adequate for most purposes as the storage capacity is limited.

Full marks would be awarded for an argument that put forward four of these points in a clear and logical way.

Free-response questions

Little use is made of free-response and open-ended questions in AS Level Computing. These types of question allow you to choose the context and to develop your own ideas. An example might be, 'Describe how you would introduce a new computer system incorporating point of sales terminals into a supermarket, taking care to minimise the disruption of day-to-day trading'. When answering this type of question it is important to plan your response and present your answer in a logical order.

Exam technique

Links from GCSE

Advanced Subsidiary Computing builds from grade C in GCSE Information technology. This study guide has been written so that you will be able to tackle AS Computing from a GCSE Information technology background.

You should not need to search for important material from GCSE Information technology because this has been included where needed in each chapter. If you have not studied Computing for some time, you should still be able to learn AS Computing using this text alone.

What are examiners looking for?

Examiners use instructions to help you to decide the length and depth of your answer. If a question does not seem to make sense, you may have misread it – read it again!

State, define, give or list

This requires a short, concise answer, often recall of material that can be learnt by rote.

Explain, describe or discuss

Some reasoning or some reference to theory is required, depending on the context.

Outline

This implies a short response, almost a list of sentences or bullet points.

Predict or deduce

You are not expected to answer by recall but by making a connection between pieces of information.

Suggest

You are expected to apply your general knowledge to a 'novel' situation, one which you have not directly studied during the AS Computing course.

Calculate

This is used when a numerical answer is required. You should always use units in quantities and significant figures should be used with care.

Look to see how many significant figures have been used for quantities in the question and give your answer to this degree of accuracy.

If the question uses 3 significant figures, then give your answer to 3 significant figures also.

Some dos and don'ts

Dos

Do answer the question.

• No credit can be given for a good answer that is irrelevant to the question.

Do use the mark allocation to guide how much you write.

- Two marks are awarded for two valid points – writing more will rarely gain more credit and could mean wasted time or even contradicting earlier valid points.

Do use diagrams, equations and tables in your responses.

- Even in 'essay-type' questions, these offer an excellent way of communicating Computing.

Do write legibly.

- An examiner cannot give marks if the answer cannot be read.

Do write using correct spelling and grammar. Structure longer essays carefully.

- Marks are now awarded for the quality of your language in exams.

Don'ts

Don't fill up any blank space on a paper.

- In structured questions, the number of dotted lines should guide the length of your answer.
- If you write too much, you waste time and may not finish the exam paper. You also risk contradicting yourself.

Don't write out the question again.

- This wastes time. The marks are for the answer!

Don't contradict yourself.

- The examiner cannot be expected to choose which answer is intended.

Don't spend too much time on a part that you find difficult.

- You may not have enough time to complete the exam. You can always return to a difficult calculation if you have time at the end of the exam.

What grade do you want?

Everyone would like to improve their grades but you will only manage this with a lot of hard work and determination. You should have a fair idea of your natural ability and likely grade in Computing and the hints below offer advice on improving that grade.

For a Grade A

You will need to be a very good all-rounder.

You must go into every exam knowing the work extremely well.

You must be able to apply your knowledge to new, unfamiliar situations.

You need to have practiced many, many exam questions so that you are ready for the type of question that will appear.

The exams test all areas of the syllabus and any weaknesses in your knowledge will be found out. There must be no holes in your knowledge and understanding. For a Grade A, you must be competent in all areas.

For a Grade C

You must have a reasonable grasp of Computing but you may have weaknesses in several areas and you will be unsure of some of the reasons for the answers.

Many Grade C candidates are just as good at answering questions as the Grade A students but holes and weaknesses often show up in just some topics.

To improve, you will need to master your weaknesses and you must prepare thoroughly for the exam. You must become a better all-rounder.

For a Grade E

You cannot afford to miss the easy marks. Even if you find Computing difficult to understand and would be happy with a Grade E, there are plenty of questions in which you can gain marks.

You must memorise all definitions.

You must practise exam questions to give yourself confidence that you do know how to answer them. In exams, answer the parts of questions that you know first. You must not waste time on the difficult parts. You can always go back to these later.

The areas of Computing that you find most difficult are going to be hard to score on in exams. Even in the difficult questions, there are still marks to be gained. Show your working in calculations because credit is given for a sound method. You can always gain some marks if you get part of the way towards the solution.

What marks do you need?

The table below shows how your average mark is transferred into a grade.

average	80%	70%	60%	50%	40%
grade	A	B	C	D	E

Four steps to successful revision

Step 1: Understand

- Study the topic to be learned slowly. Make sure you understand the logic or important concepts.
- Mark up the text if necessary – underline, highlight and make notes.
- Re-read each paragraph slowly.

GO TO STEP 2

Step 2: Summarise

- Now make your own revision note summary:
  What is the main idea, theme or concept to be learned?
  What are the main points? How does the logic develop?
  Ask questions: Why? How? What next?
- Use bullet points, mind maps, patterned notes.
- Link ideas with mnemonics, mind maps, crazy stories.
- Note the title and date of the revision notes
  (e.g. Computing: File processing, 3rd March).
- Organise your notes carefully and keep them in a file.

This is now in **short term memory**. You will forget 80% of it if you do not go to Step 3.
GO TO STEP 3, but first take a 10 minute break.

Step 3: Memorise

- Take 25 minute learning 'bites' with 5 minute breaks.
- After each 5 minute break test yourself:
  Cover the original revision note summary.
  Write down the main points.
  Speak out loud (record on tape).
  Tell someone else.
  Repeat many times.

The material is well on its way to **long term memory**.
You will forget 40% if you do not do step 4. **GO TO STEP 4**

Step 4: Track/Review

- Create a Revision Diary (one A4 page per day).
- Make a revision plan for the topic, e.g. 1 day later, 1 week later, 1 month later.
- Record your revision in your Revision Diary, e.g.
  Computing: File processing, 3rd March 25 minutes
  Computing: File processing, 5th March 15 minutes
  Computing: File processing, 3rd April 15 minutes
  ... and then at monthly intervals.

Chapter 1

Applications of computers

The following topics are covered in this chapter:

- *Types of application*
- *Application software*
- *Implications*

1.1 Types of application

After studying this section you should be able to:

- *recall the major applications of computers*
- *appreciate where computers might be used*

The range of applications

AQA	M2
EDEXCEL	M1
OCR	M3
WJEC	CP2

Computers are applied to almost every walk of life. The first applications to be computerised were in the area of accounting (banking, payroll, company accounts) which involved a large number of repetitive tasks. As computer hardware became more affordable the range of applications expanded rapidly. You need to make yourself aware of a number of applications. The best approach to this is to improve your general knowledge of computers by reading newspapers and making a note whenever computer systems are mentioned on the radio and television. You should be prepared to answer the following questions:

You may be asked about almost any application. You can only make yourself familiar with a limited number so make sure you understand what these applications do for their users.

- What is the application used for?
- How are data captured?
- How are data processed?
- What hardware is used?
- How has this application affected the people who work in the organisation?
- How does this application affect society?
- How does the application cope with hardware or software failure?
- How does the application maintain security of the data?

> In most cases there is a cost involved in implementing a computer system, so it is necessary to show that the benefits outweigh the costs.

KEY POINT

Commercial systems

AQA	M2
EDEXCEL	M1
OCR	M3
WJEC	CP2

Commercial organisations use computer systems for many reasons. All companies face competition and so any means of gaining an advantage by using a computer must be taken if the companies are to be successful. The use of these systems is not limited to profit-making organisations as it is equally important that all organisations (charities, schools, etc.) make the best use of their resources. Computer systems offer the following advantages:

- They reduce costs by using fewer people.
- They improve accuracy by reducing the amount of manual processing.
- They process the data more quickly giving up-to-date information.
- They can provide management information in a concise form.

Applications generally fall into the following categories.

Common business applications

These are applications that perform business tasks that are common to a wide range of organisations. Typical examples are payroll, company accounts, ordering, sales.

Industry-specific applications

As well as the common business applications there is a wide range of applications that are specific to a particular organisation. Examples might be a system to manage the allocation of beds in a hospital, and banking systems to operate automated cash machines. These applications will have the same benefits as the common business applications but in addition they can provide a better service to the organisation's customers.

Control systems

AQA	M2
EDEXCEL	M1
OCR	M3
WJEC	CP2

A computer system can be used to control some mechanical device. This mechanical device can be anything from a video recorder to a jumbo jet. This means that a wide range of applications is possible.

Robots

A robot has the following hardware components:

- Sensors – to detect changes in light, temperature, pressure, movement, and so on.
- Analogue-to-digital converters – to convert the analogue signals produced by the sensors into digital signals that can be processed by the computer.
- Actuators – to provide mechanical movement.
- A microprocessor – to process the data.

Robots can be used to replace a human operator giving the following advantages:

- They will perform routine repetitive tasks without getting tired or making mistakes.
- They will work for 24 hours a day.
- They can produce a better quality product than is humanly possible.
- They can be used in dangerous places.

Embedded systems

It is common practice to replace complex mechanical control systems with computer-controlled systems, for example a washing machine controller. This type of system is called an **embedded system**.

When a small light control generates a large mechanical advantage (for example the throttle control on a motor car) it is called a servo system. It is becoming the trend to replace servo systems with embedded systems involving robots. Examples include the 'fly by wire' aeroplane control systems, and engine management systems in motor cars.

> Embedded systems are used to improve accuracy and reliability. They also have the advantage of not suffering as much from wear and tear.
>
> **KEY POINT**

CAD/CAM

AQA	M2
EDEXCEL	M1
OCR	M3
WJEC	CP2

Although benefits will be obtained from CAD alone the main gains to be had from this type of system come from the combination of CAD with CAM.

Computer aided design (CAD) systems allow manufacturing and construction businesses to design their products on a computer screen. It takes nearly as long to draw a design on the screen as on paper but the benefits are:

- Improved accuracy
- Reuse of existing designs
- Easy to update designs.

Modern CAD systems will allow you to design a building and then provide a three-dimensional model on the screen to allow you to see the finished building.

A **computer aided manufacturing (CAM)** system will take the CAD design and use this to directly control the machines that manufacture the part.

Expert systems

AQA	M2
EDEXCEL	M1
OCR	M3
WJEC	CP2

An **expert system** has the ability to answer questions that might otherwise need some human expert to answer. The system stores facts and rules about a particular subject. When it is given a problem it uses these facts and rules to give a response. An example of an expert system might be in the field of medical diagnosis. An expert system can store the knowledge of several experts but it does tend to be inflexible.

Artificial intelligence

AQA	M2
EDEXCEL	M1
OCR	M3
WJEC	CP2

You only need to be aware of expert systems. It is not necessary to know how they work in detail.

Artificial intelligence (AI) is a term given to computer systems that appear to be intelligent. There have been many attempts to define what is mean by intelligence and we don't need to be concerned as to its exact meaning. A genuine AI application should be able to exhibit the ability to learn as well as to produce results. We might consider the following applications to exhibit artificial intelligence:

- Handwriting recognition
- Speech recognition
- Recognising people's faces
- Language processing.

Some AI systems use a special type of processor known as a neural network. This is an attempt to mimic the way that the human brain works.

Communication systems

AQA	M2
EDEXCEL	M1
OCR	M3
WJEC	CP2

Almost any application might use communications technology to provide additional facilities.

The ability of computers to communicate with each other through networks has provided us with a range of new computer applications and allowed existing applications to develop. Examples of new applications are:

- Electronic mail – an electronic postal service
- Computer conferencing – an electronic notice board
- World Wide Web – a source of information
- E-commerce – electronic trading.

Progress check

The use of computerised systems has changed the way we work.

1 Give three applications that have affected the operation of a supermarket.
2 State an advantage to the supermarket for each application.

These three are the obvious ones, but accounts, payroll, etc. apply to any business so they can be used to obtain marks on this type of question.

1 Stock control – the automatic recording of the stock in the supermarket
  Ordering – the processing of orders for new stock
  Sales – recording of sales.
2 Stock control will provide information as to the current stock. This will prove useful for restocking shelves or providing customer information. It can also be used to determine when to reorder an item.
  Ordering will provide more accurate replenishment of stock as it can take into account the normal sales, current stock, seasonal variations.
  Sales will allow the supermarket to have an accurate record of sales.

1.2 Application software

After studying this section you should be able to:

- *describe what is meant by an applications package*
- *select suitable packages for specific tasks*
- *explain when custom-written software might be more appropriate*

LEARNING SUMMARY

Although there are a large number of application packages you need only to be familiar with word processing, spreadsheets and databases.

It is not intended that this guide should teach you all the features of the various applications. The general features are listed here, but you will have to use the various programs yourself in order to understand them properly.

Application packages

AQA	M1, M2
EDEXCEL	M1
OCR	M3
WJEC	CP1, CP2

There are a number of general-purpose programs that can often provide most or all of the requirements of an application. Such a program is called an **application package**. The most common application packages are described below.

Word processor

You will no doubt be familiar with the use of a word processing package. If you have not already done so, try out all the features described.

This package allows the user to produce documents of various types. It can produce reports, letters, essays, and so on. Modern word processors have all the features necessary to produce newspapers and magazines. Typical features of a word processor are:

- Type and correct text, delete text, move text
- Produce various layouts, set margins, organise into columns, and so on
- Set fonts and special effects, italic, bold, underline
- Insert pictures and diagrams
- Create indexes and table of contents
- Find and replace text
- Check spelling and grammar
- Automatically produce personalised letters (mail merge).

Spreadsheet

This package allows the user to enter data and to perform calculations on them. A typical use might be to keep simple accounts, like those shown in Figure 1.

The data are organised into cells that can contain data or formulae. The formulae can use numbers or the contents of other cells to perform the calculations.

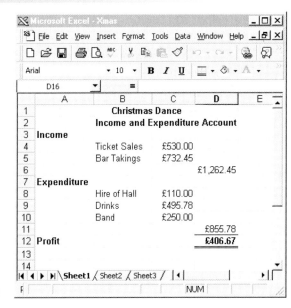

Figure 1

As with the word processor, you should try out all the features described in a spreadsheet package so that you are familiar with them.

Typical features of a spreadsheet package are:

- Enter numerical data or text
- Enter formulae that contain numerical operations
- Functions to perform mathematical or statistical calculations
- Sorting of data into sequence
- Charts of various types
- Automatically perform a series of operations using a **macro**.

Database

Again, try out these features in a database package. You will then find it straightforward to answer questions in this area.

This package stores and manipulates large quantities of data. It allows the user to enter the data and provides reports that allow the data to be viewed in different forms. Most modern database packages store the data in tables and allow the data in different tables to be related in various ways. Typical features of a database package are:

- Forms to enter the data
- Queries that allow the data to be selected and sorted in various ways
- Tabular reports
- Charts of various types.

Bespoke software

AQA	M1, M2
EDEXCEL	M1
OCR	M3
WJEC	CP1, CP2

There are packages for most situations, but it is often necessary to have an individual program written for a particular application. This is called **bespoke software** or **custom-written software**. It is more expensive to use custom-written software as the organisation has to bear all of the cost of its production, but it might be the only way to get exactly what is required. This might be because the organisation performs some task that is unusual or because it operates in an individual way.

Progress check

1 Identify two different applications in a school that might be implemented by using a spreadsheet package.
2 For each application give two features that make a spreadsheet package particularly suitable.

The features described are not the only ones that would be used. The examiner is testing you to discover whether you have thought about the problem and suggested a sensible answer.

1 Recording of marks
Preparing a school budget
(The important point here is to give two different applications. Try to avoid giving general answers like 'Accounts'. Although this might get you a mark it is difficult to get many more.)
2 Recording of marks would use formulae to calculate the total marks per pupil and would use the ability to sort data to place the pupils in rank order or alphabetical order.
Preparing a school budget would also use formulae to calculate totals and charts to present the budget to the school managers.
(Obviously there are several answers to this type of question. The suggested answer gives two fairly different applications.)

1.3 Implications

After studying this section you should be able to:

- discuss the social and economic implications of computer applications
- discuss privacy issues related to computer use
- discuss the legal implications of computer use

Social and economic implications

AQA	M2
EDEXCEL	M1
OCR	M3
WJEC	CP2

Employment issues

Computers have changed the way that we work. The introduction of computer systems has meant that some occupations have disappeared to be replaced by new ones that require different skills. This has meant that people have lost their jobs and have had to face going back to college to be retrained to do something else. Often people have not lost their jobs but have had to face new working practices, for example secretaries are now using word processing systems instead of typewriters, e-mail has replaced letters, and so on. Some people find it challenging and enjoy the changes while others are worried by them.

Health hazards

A number of health hazards associated with prolonged use of a computer have been identified:

- Eyestrain from looking at the screen
- Back problems from sitting too long in one position
- Repetitive strain injury (RSI) causing pain in the arms and wrists.

Make sure that you are aware of the general health hazards described here. Questions will often ask for a number of risks associated with the use of computers.

The European Commission has issued a directive dealing with the health hazards and laying down requirements for working with VDUs (visual display units). In the UK, the EC requirements are carried out via the Health and Safety (Display Screen Equipment) Regulations 1992 which include clauses on the following issues:

- Employees must be given regular breaks or changes in activity.
- Employers must conduct a risk analysis to evaluate the risks to eyesight, physical problems and mental stress. They must also take appropriate action to remove any risks discovered.
- The workstations must conform to certain minimum standards. These standards state the maximum radiation emissions from the screen, that the keyboard must be separate from the screen, and that the chair must be adjustable in height and tilt.

Social issues

New computer applications are appearing every day. We already depend on computers for most things that we do and in the main they have improved our standard of living. They have provided many cheap goods of high quality and enabled a range of services that would be impossible without computer systems. There are some concerns that people have about the increasing use of computers:

- Privacy – computer systems make it possible to track everything we do.
- Employment – computer systems can cause unemployment.
- Safety – computer systems control airplanes, railways, and other transport systems.
- Junk mail – it is possible to send advertising material that is not wanted.

Legal implications

AQA	M2
EDEXCEL	M1
OCR	M3
WJEC	CP2

Data Protection Act 1998

This Act, introduced in 1984 and updated in 1998, is an attempt to protect members of the public from the misuse of personal data that are held about them on computer systems. Data users must specify the purpose for storing the data. The Data Protection Act states that users of such systems should keep to the following rules:

- The data shall only be held for specified purposes.
- The data shall not be disclosed to third parties unless doing so is compatible with the specified purposes.
- Only data needed for the specified purposes shall be stored.
- The data must be kept up-to-date and accurate.
- The data must not be kept after they are needed for the specified purposes.
- The data must be kept securely.

The individual whose data are stored also has some rights under the Act:

- He/she is entitled to be informed when data are held about them.
- He/she is entitled to access any data held about them. (The data user may charge for this.)
- He/she is entitled to have any errors in the data corrected or erased.

Computer Misuse Act 1990

> A popular question with examiners is to ask for the details of these Acts, so it is worth your while to become familiar with their principles.

The Computer Misuse Act introduced three new offences:

- unauthorised access to computer material
- unauthorised access with intent to commit or facilitate commission of further offences
- unauthorised modification of computer material.

The first offence might be regarded as hacking, that is looking at information that has been protected with passwords. The second offence relates to using the information from a computer system to help with a different crime such as fraud or blackmail. The third offence relates to a hacker who illegally gains access to some data and then proceeds to alter the data.

Progress check

> Questions in this area often ask you to recall various features of the Act. If you can't remember the Act exactly do not despair. Describe what you think it is. The examiner will not be expecting to receive the exact wording of the Act.

Give three categories of crime identified under the Computer Misuse Act.

1 Unauthorised access to computer material (hacking).
2 Unauthorised access with intent to commit or facilitate commission of further offences, for example unauthorised copying.
3 Unauthorised modification of computer material, for example introducing a virus.

People in IT

EDEXCEL   M1

The computing industry is still evolving and new jobs appear regularly as changes in technology allow new tasks to be performed. Current jobs available include the following:

- Systems analysis
- Programming
- Testing
- Database administration
- Network administration
- Website administration
- Computer manufacture
- Sales
- System support
- Data entry.

> You should be aware of the general types of jobs that are available in the IT profession. You may be able to use this knowledge in many questions about the application of computers.

Systems analysis

The systems analyst will analyse, design, document, implement and test a computer system.

Programming

Once an analyst has specified a computer system it may be necessary to write some computer programs. A computer programmer writes, tests and documents computer programs as specified by the analyst. There are two main types of computer programmers.

- Application programmers – who develop application programs.
- Systems programmers – who develop operating systems and associated programs.

> Analysts, programmers and testers make up a typical system development team.

Testing

Testers are employed to test computer systems to discover faults that remain after they have been debugged and tested by the development team.

Database administration

A database administrator (DBA) is employed to design and implement a database. The DBA will maintain the database to ensure that adequate backup copies are kept and that the database continues to function satisfactorily.

Network administration

The network administrator will be involved in setting up computer networks and maintaining the necessary software and hardware.

Website administration

> The administrators are involved in the day-to-day use of a computer system.

The Website administrator will design and install the necessary hardware and software to provide a website. They will also be responsible for the backup and maintenance of the site.

Computer manufacture

There are many jobs available in the manufacture of computers, from the manufacture of the components to the assembly of the finished product.

Sales

This involves the marketing and sale of computer hardware and software. The various items to be sold include:

Complete computer systems

Electronic components – memory, power supplies, etc.

Peripherals – printers, scanners, etc.

System Software – operating systems, etc.

Application packages – word processors, databases, etc.

System support

This can involve hardware support or software support. The hardware specialist will repair or replace faulty components. The software specialist will install and maintain the software that is used on the computer system. There will often be a help desk that will provide the first contact for a customer with a problem.

Data entry

Large numbers of staff are involved in entering data into a computer system. The data may be entered from forms that have been completed manually but, increasingly, the data for a transaction is entered as the transaction takes place (e.g. point of sales terminals).

Progress check

When an organisation wishes to introduce a new computer system a number of different people will be employed. Describe the role of three different types of staff that might be involved.

1 The systems analyst will analyse, design, document, implement and test a computer system.

2 Once an analyst has specified a computer system it may be necessary to write some computer programs. A computer programmer writes, tests and documents computer programs as specified by the analyst.

3 Testers are employed to test computer systems to discover faults that remain after they have been debugged and tested by the development team.

Sample questions and model answers

1

Word processing and desktop publishing software are being used in the home and in business to produce well-presented documents. Advantages to the user over non-computerised methods include the ease of error correction, and the range of formatting and presentation techniques available.

(a) Give **three** further advantages to the user. [3]

(a) Wizards or templates are provided for some standard types of documents.
It is easy to import text from other applications.
A mail merge facility to enable the production of a personalised mail shot.

(b) Give **one** reason why some people regret this trend. [1]

AEB 1999, Paper 2

(b) Manual skills such as typesetting have become devalued.

2

Tifpeek Ltd operates sports and leisure clubs in a number of towns and cities throughout the country. Each provides a wide range of fitness, sporting and health facilities for its members. Members can use and book the facilities of their own club or of any other Tifpeek clubs. Membership is renewed annually. Each club also provides its members with a wide range of catering and shopping facilities.

Tifpeek's accountants, in their annual report, advise that the company's accounts be computerised. There are a number of accounts packages available 'off the shelf'. The management of Tifpeek have to decide between using an off-the-shelf accounts package and a tailor-made piece of software.

(a) Explain clearly the differences between off-the-shelf software and tailor-made software. [4]

(a) Off-the-shelf software is a general package which must normally be adapted to suit the application. In this example it would probably be a spreadsheet. Tailor-made software is specially written for the task or organisation. No adaptation should be necessary.

(b) Describe and discuss **three** advantages of each of these two approaches to the company. [8]

OCR Specimen

(b) • Off-the-shelf products are tried and tested.
• They are also immediately available.
• Existing users can be contacted and asked their opinion of the product.
• The system can be seen in operation.
• An off-the shelf product should be relatively cheap as the development costs can be shared amongst the users.
• Training in its use might be available cheaply.
• A tailor-made solution is specially designed so that it should do exactly what is required.
• Minimal changes to the current operating procedures should be possible.
• Future user-specific modifications should be possible.

Practice examination questions

1 Many governments have passed laws which restrict the uses that may be made of data stored in computers.

Identify the problems that such legislation is designed to overcome, and describe the main features of the legislation which cover these problems. [6]

EDEXCEL

2 Give **three** rights of the data subject under the Data Protection Act. [3]

NEAB 1998, CPO2

3 Suppose you had moved house three years ago and have recently been receiving mail for the previous owners advertising water sports equipment. The previous owners tell you that they had entered a competition to win a scuba diving holiday about four years ago but had not won. Presumably, the competition organisers had passed on their name and address to the (independent) water sports company, although they had indicated on the form that they did not wish this to happen.

Give two principles of the Data Protection legislation which would appear to have been broken here. [2]

AEB 1999, Paper 2

4 It is now possible for office staff to work from home using a computer and a telephone link to access other members of their company and the company's computer system.

(a) Give **four** benefits to the employee of this method of working. [4]

(b) Give **two** benefits to society of this method of working. [2]

NEAB 1998, CPO2

5 The publisher of a local daily newspaper has purchased a network of microcomputers for its office. The publisher has adopted the strategy of commissioning a software house to produce software with which the team of journalists can produce the newspaper.

(a) Apart from standard features such as editing of text, style of text (e.g. bold and italic), saving and printing, describe and justify **three** features that the publisher could specify for the software. [6]

(b) (i) Instead of commissioning new software, give **one** alternative strategy available to the publisher. [1]

(ii) State **one** argument in favour of **each** strategy. [2]

NEAB 1998, CPO2

Chapter 2

Computer hardware

The following topics are covered in this chapter:

- *Internal components of a computer system*
- *Storage devices*
- *Input/output devices*

2.1 Internal components of a computer system

After studying this section you should be able to:

- identify the internal components of a computer system
- describe the fetch/execute cycle
- explain how data flow around a computer system

LEARNING SUMMARY

System components

AQA	M1
EDEXCEL	M1
OCR	M1
WJEC	CP2

The internal components are normally placed on the motherboard of a desktop computer.

The internal components of a computer system are:

- Processor – the part of the computer system that executes the programs
- Memory – high-speed storage for programs and data
- Interfaces – to connect external devices (called peripherals)
- Clock – to provide timing signals
- Buses – to connect together all of the above into a computer system.

Buses

A **system bus** is simply a number of wires that are used to connect devices together in such a way as to allow data or control information to pass from device to device. The system bus will normally consist of three buses:

- Data bus
- Address bus
- Control bus.

A typical system is illustrated in Figure 2.

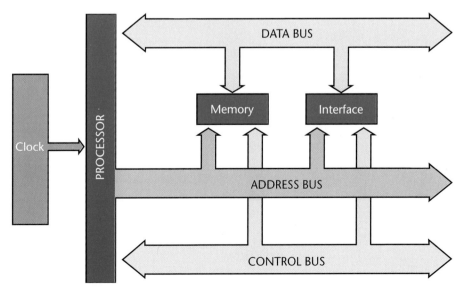

Figure 2

You should be aware of the effect of changing the size (sometimes called the width) of the data bus and/or the address bus.

The data bus is used to transfer data from one device to another. Each wire in the data bus transfers one binary digit (**bit**), so the number of wires determines the amount of data that can be transferred at one time.

Each part of the system is numbered. We call this number the **address**. The address bus carries addresses, i.e. it carries a number that identifies a particular part of the system. Most addresses apply to memory locations but it is also possible to address an interface. Each wire carries a binary digit (bit) and the number of wires in the address bus determines the amount of memory that can be used in the system. A 16 bit address bus will allow 65536 (64k) addresses, a 32 bit address bus will allow 4 294 967 296 (4 gig) addresses, etc.

The control bus carries signals that control the operation of each device. There will be a clock signal to provide synchronisation. There will be control signals that command the memory to read or write and numerous other signals to ensure that the system operates successfully.

> The bus system determines the size of each memory location and it also determines how much memory can be installed in the system.

Processor

The processor is the part of the computer that executes the program that is stored in the memory. The processor has three main components:

- Control unit
- Arithmetic and logic unit (ALU)
- Registers.

The control unit controls the rest of the processor by generating appropriate control signals. The ALU performs arithmetic operations and the registers are a small number of read/write memory cells that operate at very high speed.

When the computer is turned on it starts performing what is known as the fetch/execute cycle. The main memory will have coded program instructions and the purpose of the fetch/execute cycle is to execute these instructions. To assist in this process one of the registers is used exclusively to keep track of the memory address of the next instruction. This register is often called the **program counter**.

The fetch/execute cycle consists of the following steps:

1 The processor copies the contents of the program counter on the address bus and requests that the memory be read.
2 The processor reads the data bus that now contains the instruction to be decoded and stores it in the instruction register.
3 The processor executes the instruction and increments the program counter.

In this manner the processor works its way through any program that is stored in the main memory. The speed of the processor is controlled by the speed of the clock. The width of the buses and the size and number of the registers will affect the complexity of the instructions that the processor can execute.

> The processor is the heart of the computer system. The power of a processor is controlled by the clock speed and the complexity of the instructions it is able to execute.

Clock

The clock is a simple electronic device that produces a pulse of electricity at regular intervals. It is used to synchronise the computer system. The clock is normally connected to the processor that passes on synchronising signals through the control bus.

> **KEY POINT**
>
> Clock speeds are usually measured in megahertz (MHz);
> • 1 MHz is 1 million clock signals every second.

Memory

A computer's memory is normally organised into memory locations. A memory location is a fixed amount of memory that has an address. The address is simply a number that can be used to allow immediate access to any memory location.

When the processor wishes to access a memory location it places the memory location's address on the address bus and sends appropriate control signals via the control bus.

The terms 'byte' and 'word' are often misused. You will find the term 'byte' is used less and less as most computers have at least 16 bits in a memory location. It is nevertheless a popular term with examiners.

If a memory location contains 8 binary digits (bits) it is known as a byte. If it contains more than 8 bits (typically 16, 32, 64 or 128 bits) it is known as a word.

Read only memory

Some of the computer's memory is known as read only memory (or ROM). The contents of ROM cannot be changed by the processor. When the computer is turned off the contents of ROM are maintained so that it still has the same information when you turn the computer back on again. This type of memory is known as non-volatile.

The bootstrap program is the first program to be executed whenever the computer system is switched on.

ROM is used for the following purposes:
• To store the bootstrap program that starts the computer.
• To store fixed data associated with the computer system.
• Sometimes to store programs that remain in the computer at all times, for example a palmtop may have all its programs stored in ROM.

Random access memory

All memory is random access in that it can be accessed randomly, but the name random access memory (or RAM) is given to the memory that can be written to. It should really be called read/write memory. When the computer is switched off the contents of RAM are lost. For this reason RAM is known as volatile memory.

Most of the memory in a computer system will be RAM.

RAM is used for the following purposes:

• To store programs that are being executed.
• To store data that are required for immediate use.
• As buffers for external storage devices.

Cache memory

Many computer systems have special high-speed memory that is known as cache memory. This may be either a part of the processor or a special high-speed cache memory chip. It is used to speed up the execution of computer programs. The following may be stored in cache memory:

• Program instructions that are executed many times
• Regularly used data

Pipelining is a hardware feature that speeds up the execution of program instructions.

• Virtual memory page tables (see System software chapter)
• Pipelining.

> **KEY POINT**
>
> Cache memory is faster than RAM and ROM but it is slower to access than a register.

Interfaces

In order to connect external devices (printers, keyboards, disks, and so on) to the system, interfaces are required. An interface is able to communicate with the buses of the system and also with the external devices. The external devices will use different protocols (a protocol is a set of rules that specify how the device will communicate) from the rest of the computer system. The interface will provide the following features:

- The external device will normally operate at a much lower speed than the buses.
- The external device may use a different voltage.
- The interface will convert signals from one protocol to the other.
- The interface will provide electrical protection from faulty devices.

An interface will consist of:

- Electronics to connect to the system bus.
- Electronics to connect to the cable that goes to the device.
- Data registers to hold the data being transferred.
- Control register to allow commands to be passed to the interface.
- Status register to provide information about the current state of the device.

Do not confuse these hardware interfaces with the human/computer interface.

> Interfaces are needed in order to connect peripherals. Peripherals consist of such devices as printers, screens, keyboards, mice and disk drives.

KEY POINT

Progress check

1 A computer system consists of a processor, 128 Mbytes of main memory and 2 Kbytes of cache memory. Give **two** methods of increasing the power of such a system. For **each** method describe how it will improve the system.
2 RAM and ROM are two types of memory. Give a use for each type of memory and explain why it is suitable.

1 Increase the clock speed. This will cause the processor to execute instructions more quickly. Increase the amount of cache. This will speed up the execution by allowing more instructions to be executed from cache.

2 RAM can be used to store programs that are being executed. It is suitable as the programs can be loaded into RAM as it is a read/write memory.
ROM can be used to store the bootstrap program. ROM is non-volatile so the program will always be available when the computer is turned on.
[Note that alternative answers are that RAM can store data temporarily. ROM can store data about the system.]

2.2 Storage devices

After studying this section you should be able to:

- describe the different types of storage device
- compare and contrast different storage devices
- give appropriate uses for different devices

LEARNING SUMMARY

General description

AQA	M1, M2
EDEXCEL	M1
OCR	M1
WJEC	CP2

Generally the larger the buffer the faster the data transfer but the buffer size may be limited by the amount of memory available and/or the physical characteristics of the storage device.

Storage devices are a non-volatile form of storage, i.e. the contents are not lost when the computer is turned off. The data are stored logically in the form of files and a file contains a number of records. As a result, information about the files must also be stored on the storage device in a special area known as the **directory**. File processing is described later in the book. The purpose of this section is to explain the physical characteristics of the various devices.

Data are transferred to and from storage devices in **blocks**. A block can be anything from about 128 bytes to tens of thousands of bytes. A block of data is transferred continuously at the speed of the storage device to or from the memory of the computer. The name given to memory allocated to this purpose is a **buffer**.

Magnetic disk

AQA	M1, M2
EDEXCEL	M1
OCR	M1
WJEC	CP2

It is the ability to obtain data from any part of the disk very quickly that has made the disk such a popular storage device.

The magnetic disk is covered in a magnetic material that can be used to store data in the form of binary digits (bits). In order to read or write the data the disk is spun and a read/write head moves over the surface. When data are read from or written to the disk the head remains stationary. In this way data are stored in a track that forms a circle of data (see Figure 3). The read/write head can be moved to different positions to allow it to write to different tracks.

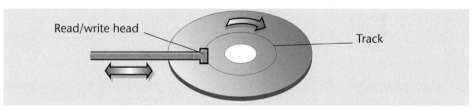

Figure 3

Tracks are subdivided into sectors and a sector is the amount of data that is read or written to a disk each time it is accessed. The tracks and sectors are both numbered (see Figure 4). In this way the data can be stored in a particular place on the disk by using the track and sector number as a disk address.

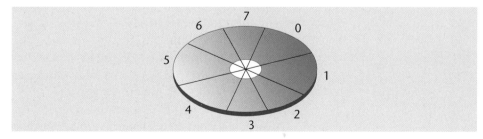

Figure 4 A disk with eight sectors numbered 0 to 7

There are two main types of magnetic disk.

Hard disk

The hard disk is made from aluminium. It is normally supplied as a sealed unit and will often consist of a number of disks on a common spindle. All the heads will be connected together so that they all move together. The tracks that are directly above and below each other can be read or written without moving the heads. This set of tracks is known as a cylinder (see Figure 5).

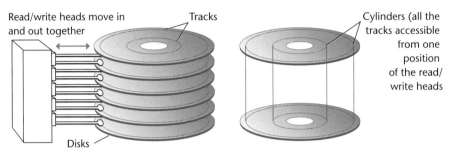

Figure 5

The hard disk has become the main storage device for storing the software of a computer system and it is also the preferred device for storing databases and other company data that are required immediately.

The address of a sector of data on such a disk now becomes a surface number, a cylinder number and a sector number.

The hard disk is capable of holding large amounts of data and it has a very high data transfer rate.

Floppy disk

A floppy disk is made from soft plastic and is placed in a hard plastic case. A floppy disk holds a limited amount of data and has a relatively slow data transfer rate. It does have the advantage of being very portable and can therefore be used to pass a small amount of data from one system to another. It can also be used to take a copy of small amounts of data.

As it has such a low capacity and low transfer speed the floppy disk is used only for storing small amounts of data. It is used on PCs and other small desktop systems, but will not normally be found on larger systems.

> **KEY POINT**
> The magnetic disk is the main storage medium for current computers. The reasons for this are its high storage capacity, high transfer rate and its ability to access any part of the disk directly.

Magnetic tape

AQA	M1, M2
EDEXCEL	M1
OCR	M1, M2
WJEC	CP2

Magnetic tape consists of a soft plastic tape covered in a magnetic material. Some mainframe systems may have large reels of tape, but generally tape is supplied in the form of a cartridge. Magnetic tape is a cheap, robust form of data storage and can hold large amounts of data.

Data are stored in the form of blocks. A block is the amount of data that is transferred at any one time. In order to read or write data the tape must be moving past the read/write heads at a certain speed, but when the data transfer is completed the tape has to stop. It is not possible to start and stop the tape instantly so a gap is left between blocks to allow the tape to accelerate and decelerate. This is known as the **inter block gap**. It is advantageous to use as large a block as possible to minimise these interblock gaps as this will reduce the amount of wasted space on the tape and also speed up the data transfer with fewer stops. A block will normally contain a number of records (see Figure 6).

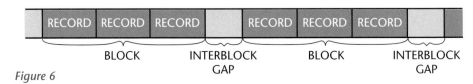

Figure 6

Do not make the mistake of thinking that magnetic tape is slower than magnetic disk.

The data transfer rate is comparable to that of a hard disk but the data cannot be accessed directly. In order to find data on a tape the computer has to read all the data up to the required block. This limits the use of tape, and these days it is normally used for the following purposes:

- Backup – keeping copies of important data
- Archiving – keeping large amounts of data that might be needed in the future
- Transporting data from one system to another
- Distributing software.

> The main use for magnetic tapes is as a backup medium. As a result there is more data stored on magnetic tape than there is on magnetic disk.
>
> **KEY POINT**

Optical disk

AQA	M1, M2
EDEXCEL	M1
OCR	M1
WJEC	CP2

Just because CDROMs are faster than floppy disks does not make them fast. Do not forget that magnetic tapes are much faster and hold more data.

An optical disk is a hard plastic disk that has a mirrored surface. The data are stored by removing the mirroring with a laser. The early optical disks could only be written once and then became read only devices. This type of optical disk is known as a WORM (write once read many) disk.

The most common form of optical disk is known as a CD and uses similar protocols to music CDs. When these disks are supplied with the data already written on them they are known as CDROMs. It is now possible to obtain magneto-optical disks that can be overwritten.

Optical disks have a storage capacity that is greater than a floppy disk but much less than a magnetic tape or a hard disk. They are also faster than a floppy but slower than a tape or hard disk. Common uses for optical disks are:

- To distribute software
- To distribute information, for example, encyclopaedias and directories
- Backup – keeping copies of important data.

> Optical disks have limited storage and are comparatively slow, but the fact that they are often read only has made them a popular means of distributing software and multimedia information.
>
> **KEY POINT**

Progress check

As the question refers to magnetic disks and floppy disks it is clear that a magnetic disk is in fact a hard disk. If you are not told otherwise it is usually safe to assume that a magnetic disk is a hard disk.

Give an appropriate use for each of the following storage devices. In each case give reasons for your choice.

1 Magnetic disk.
2 Floppy disk.
3 Magnetic tape.
4 Optical disk.

1 A magnetic disk could be used to hold the software for the system. It is suitable as it has a large storage capacity, provides direct access to the software and is immediately available. [An equally good case could be made for storing a database.]
2 A floppy disk could be used to transport documents from one computer system to another. A floppy disk is portable and, although it has limited capacity, will be able to store a moderately large document.
3 A magnetic tape could be used to backup the hard disk. It has a large capacity and a high data transfer rate. It is also a cheap form of storage.
4 An optical disk might be used to distribute software. It is portable and it has a reasonable capacity. It is also read only, so the software cannot be corrupted.

2.3 Input/output devices

After studying this section you should be able to:

- describe the range of input/output devices
- give appropriate uses for different input/output devices

Common devices

AQA	M2
EDEXCEL	M1
OCR	M1
WJEC	CP2

There is a large range of input and output devices including many specialist devices, for example a cash dispenser. This section attempts to describe the common devices that are likely to be found attached to a computer system. The specialist devices are generally made up from these common devices.

Keyboard

Still the most popular method of input despite a poor design (it was in fact designed to slow down typists). Various attempts have been made to improve the design of the keyboard but they have all failed.

A keyboard converts key depressions into character codes. Every time a key is depressed the keyboard generates a set of binary digits that correspond to the character on the key. Keyboards are used in a large number of applications to input data and in most cases the data entered are stored on a magnetic disk. This is known as a key to disk data entry system.

Mouse

Another poor design but still very popular. Various replacements have been tried but none has proved completely successful. It is easy to forget that the mouse is an input device when answering questions in this area.

A mouse is a common input device that is used in conjunction with a WIMP (windows, icons, mouse, pointer) environment. The window on the screen of the computer has a pointer (cursor) that moves when the mouse is moved. The mouse also has two or three buttons that can be pressed. The combination of these features has allowed a number of WIMP environments to be produced and they have made it much easier for a non-specialist to use a computer system.

Touch sensitive screen

A touch sensitive surface is placed in front of a screen. The surface is able to detect when and where it is touched. In this manner it is possible for a user to point to an object on a screen without the use of a mouse. These devices are to be found in information systems, for example in a tourist information centre.

Bar code scanner

When a bar code appears on an item in a supermarket (say a tin of beans) it identifies the product to enable a store's computer to recognise it at the checkout.

Bar codes consist of a series of printed stripes that can be read either backwards or forwards. The scanner passes a light beam (often a laser for greater accuracy) over the bar code and detects the pattern of light and dark stripes. Bar codes can be printed onto almost anything as they do not require high quality printing and they are now on very many goods.

Magnetic stripe reader

Small lengths of magnetic material (called magnetic stripes) can be attached to plastic cards. These magnetic stripes can be read by passing them through a magnetic stripe reader. The cards can be used for a variety of applications where you may wish to identify the carrier of the plastic card. Examples are:

- Credit cards
- Library cards
- Magnetic key locks (to allow entry to a room or building)
- Clock machines (to allow employees to clock in and out of work).

Magnetic stripe cards are gradually being replaced by smart cards. A smart card is a card that has an embedded processor as well as some memory. These can hold much more data than a stripe card and are more difficult to forge.

Scanner

> The scanner is able to detect the pattern of dots that make up the page being scanned. This set of dots is then passed to some software that makes sense of it.

A scanner 'looks at' a piece of paper and converts the image on the paper into a binary pattern. Computer systems can store the image as black and white, shades of grey or full colour. These images can then be used in a variety of applications where an image will improve the output.

Optical mark reader

> An optical mark reader is a scanner with appropriate software. It can only work with preprinted forms that have specific spaces for the user to fill in.

An optical mark reader is able to scan a piece of paper and detect where marks have been made inside preprinted boxes. This can be used for a variety of applications where the requirement is to select a particular value from a range of options. Examples include:

- Multiple-choice question papers
- National census
- National Lottery
- Football pools.

Optical character reader

> Like the optical mark reader, the optical character reader is a scanner with software that enables the computer system to recognise the characters.

The optical character reader (OCR) scans a document and is able to convert the image into characters. It literally reads the characters. This is much more accurate if the characters are printed, but some OCRs are able to read handwriting. Examples are:

- Reading postcodes on letters
- Meter readings can be written by meter reader and subsequently scanned
- Scanning documents to be used in word processing
- Hand-held devices where no keyboard is provided.

Magnetic ink character recognition

The banks have developed this system to allow the automatic processing of cheques. Each cheque has its account details encoded using magnetic ink. The magnetism can be detected by the magnetic ink character reader that 'reads' the cheque after it has been paid into a bank. This system is difficult to forge as it requires special magnetic ink.

Speech synthesiser

With the addition of a loudspeaker it is possible to create speech. The computer can generate appropriate sounds directly from the words that are stored in the computer. It is also possible to record sounds from a microphone and subsequently play them back. Examples of its use include:

- Digital telephone answering machine
- Translation systems (for example, from English to German)
- Systems for the blind
- Computer games.

Printer

Laser printers give the best results in black and white but are very expensive in colour. Generally the inkjet printer is the most popular owing to its low price and high print quality. It is really only suitable for small amounts of printing, owing to its slow speed and the high cost of ink.

Printers come in many forms. The quality can vary as can the speed. The following table sets out the most common printers and their features.

Name	Speed	Quality	Colour or black & white	Purchase price	Running costs
InkJet	Slow	Good	Colour	Cheap	Expensive
Dot matrix	Slow	Poor	Black & white	Cheap	Cheap
Laser	Fast	Excellent	Black & white	Expensive	Medium

Microfilm

It is possible to output directly onto photographic film. This can be in the form of a film that is on a reel or in the form of small sheets of thick film known as **Microfiches**. These films can then be viewed using a microfilm or a microfiche reader. This type of output is used in the same manner as printed output but it is possible to place a large amount of output onto a small amount of film.

Progress check

Suggest an appropriate input device for each of the following:

1 A system to provide information to visitors to a cathedral.
2 A system to check football pools.
3 A machine for sorting mail.
4 A cash-dispensing machine.

In each case give reasons for your choice.

1 A touch-sensitive screen would be the best choice. It will enable the system to provide a menu that can easily be selected without the need to use a keyboard or a mouse.
2 Optical mark recognition would be used to check football pools. The customer fills in boxes on the football coupon that can be automatically read by the optical mark reader.
3 Optical character recognition will be used. The optical character reader will read the postcodes from the mail and sort them for delivery.
4 A magnetic stripe will be placed on a cash card to identify the customer. The card is portable and difficult to forge.

Sample questions and model answers

1

Although large disk storage devices are now readily available for computer systems, the use of magnetic tape is still widespread. Describe two distinct uses of magnetic tape and explain its suitability in each case. [4]

EDEXCEL

You need to find situations where a tape would be used in preference to a disk.

1 Magnetic tapes can be used to backup data files in a computer system. They are particularly suitable owing to their high speed, large capacity and low cost.

Magnetic tapes can be used to transport data from one computer system to another. They are more portable and less likely to be corrupted than magnetic disks.

2

Name and briefly describe the purpose of **three** buses found within a computer. [6]

NEAB 1999, CPO2

This is a standard question that appears regularly in examinations. You need to be clear as to the purpose of the three buses.

2 The data bus is used to carry data between the processor and the other parts of the computer system.

The address bus carries numerical addresses that identify individual locations in the computer system's memory.

The control bus carries synchronisation signals to enable the various devices to co-operate in carrying out a task.

3

Give two reasons why interfaces are needed between peripheral devices and the central processor (CPU). [2]

As there are only 2 marks available you need to give 2 of these 4 points.

3 The device may operate at different speeds to the CPU.

The interface provides electrical protection for the CPU.

The peripheral may operate at a different voltage to the CPU.

The peripheral may use different protocols to the CPU.

Practice examination questions

1 State **one** advantage and **one** disadvantage of an inkjet printer compared with a laser printer. [2]

NEAB 1997, CP02

2 (a) Define the term 'buffer' and explain its purpose. [2]
(b) Give one example. [1]

AEB 1999, Paper 2

3 When buying a personal computer, the following characteristics are considered: **processor speed**; amount of **immediate access store**; and available **backing store**. For each of these characteristics, explain how it would affect the choice. [6]

OCR 1998, 6810

4 The three main components of any computer are the processor, the memory and the input-output controller. These are linked by an address bus and a data bus. The following block diagram shows this.

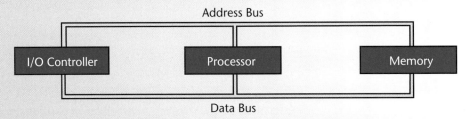

Address Bus

I/O Controller   Processor   Memory

Data Bus

(a) Copy the diagram and show clearly the directions in which signals travel along both buses. [2]
(b) Name two types of information which would be sent along the data bus. [2]
(c) What range of addresses can be accessed directly by a 16 bit address bus? [2]

AEB 1997 Paper 1

5 (a) Draw a diagram showing how the microprocessor, data bus, address bus, control bus, memory and clock are interconnected in a computer system. [4]
(b) Explain what hardware feature limits the amount of memory possible in a computer system. [2]
(c) Describe **three** hardware design changes that would increase the speed of execution of programs. [6]

NEAB 1997 CP02

Chapter 3

Data representation

The following topics are covered in this chapter:

- Number systems
- Coding of data

3.1 Number systems

After studying this section you should be able to:

- recognise numbers in binary, octal and hexadecimal
- translate binary numbers into denary, octal and hexadecimal
- translate denary numbers into binary, octal and hexadecimal
- translate hexadecimal numbers into binary and denary
- translate octal numbers into binary and denary

LEARNING SUMMARY

Binary numbers

AQA	M1
EDEXCEL	M2
OCR	M1
WJEC	CP2

Denary

The numbers in normal use are called **denary** (or base 10). The denary number system uses ten digits that are 0,1,2,3,4,5,6,7,8,9. When a number contains more than one digit each digit is worth ten times a similar digit to its immediate right. We can demonstrate this by placing the digits in columns that are labelled with their values:

100	10	1
2	5	7

Thus the number 257 would represent 2 x 100 + 5 x 10 + 7 x 1.

Binary

The **binary** number system uses just two digits, 0 and 1. A binary digit is normally referred to as a bit and each bit is worth two times the digit to its immediate right. To translate a binary number into denary we can place the bits in columns that are labelled with their values:

8	4	2	1
1	1	0	1

Thus the binary number 1101 would represent
1 x 8 + 1 x 4 + 0 x 2 + 1 x 1 = 8 + 4 + 1 = 13.

> All computer systems store data in a binary form. This is because they are composed of electronic components that can have one of only two states, for example on or off.

KEY POINT

Translating denary to binary

To translate a denary number to binary you should do the following:

1 Write down the column headings for the binary number, starting with the right-hand column. You continue to add columns until you get to the column that has a value greater than the denary number.

2 You place a 0 in this column.

3 You now process each column from left to right. If the denary number to be translated is greater than or equal to the column heading, place a 1 in the column and subtract the value of the column from the denary value. If the denary value is smaller than the column heading you simply place a zero in the column.

Take as an example the denary value 87. We write down the column headings, starting with 1, until we get to a number greater than 87. In this case it is 128.

	128	64	32	16	8	4	2	1
Place a 0 in the first column	0							
87 > 64 so place 1 in the column	0	1						
Subtract 64 from 87 giving 23								
23 < 32 so place 0 in the column	0	1	0					
23 > 16 so place a 1 in the column	0	1	0	1				
Subtract 16 from 23 giving 7								
7 < 8 so place 0 in column	0	1	0	1	0			
7 > 4 so place a 1 in the column	0	1	0	1	0	1		
Subtract 4 from 7 giving 3								
3 > 2 so place a 1 in the column	0	1	0	1	0	1	1	
Subtract 2 from 3 giving 1								
1 = 1 so place a 1 in the column	0	1	0	1	0	1	1	1
Subtract 1 from 1 giving 0								

> You can check the value is correct by converting it back to its original form.

There are no more columns to be filled so the binary number is: 01010111 (or 1010111).

> **KEY POINT**
> Values will often be shown with leading 0s. This is usually because they have to fit into a certain amount of memory.

Hexadecimal numbers

AQA	A2
OCR	M1

> Hexadecimal is the most popular method of displaying the binary data stored in a computer.

Hexadecimal

The **hexadecimal** number system uses 16 digits that are: 0, 1, 2, 3, 4, 5, 6, 7, 8, 9, A, B, C, D, E, F. Each digit is worth 16 times a similar digit to its immediate right. To translate a hexadecimal number into denary we can place the digits in columns that are labelled with their values:

256	16	1
1	C	5

As C represents twelve the hexadecimal number 1C5 would represent
1 x 256 + 12 x 16 + 5 x 1 = 256 + 192 + 5 = 453

Translating binary to hexadecimal

Divide the binary number into groups of four digits (starting from the rightmost digit). You now convert each group of four digits into a single hexadecimal digit.

In order to convert	0110111110010111			
divide the number into groups of four giving	0110	1111	1001	0111
the hexadecimal number becomes	6	F	9	7

To translate from hexadecimal to binary you simply reverse the process. To translate 1A5 we convert each hexadecimal digit into four bits:

1	A	5
0001	1010	0101

giving 000110100101 (or 110100101).

Translating denary to hexadecimal

To translate a denary number to hexadecimal you should do the following:

1 Write down the column headings for the hexadecimal number, starting with the right-hand column. You continue to add columns until you get to the column that has a value greater than the denary number.
2 You place a 0 in this column.
3 You now process each column from left to right. Divide the denary number by the column heading. The result is placed in the column and the remainder becomes the denary number still to be translated.

Take as an example the denary value 421. We write down the column headings, starting with 1, until we get to a number greater than 421. In this case it is 4096.

	4096	256	16	1
Place a 0 in the first column	0			
Divide 421 by 256 = 1 remainder 165				
Place 1 in the column, remaining value is 165	0	1		
Divide 165 by 16 = 10 remainder 5				
Place A in the column, remaining value is 5	0	1	A	
Divide 5 by 1 = 5 remainder 0				
Place 5 in the column	0	1	A	5

giving 01 (or 1).

You can avoid translating directly from denary to hexadecimal by translating first to binary and then translating the binary value to hexadecimal.

> **KEY POINT**
>
> Hexadecimal is a convenient method of displaying and entering a value that is stored in the computer in binary.

Octal numbers

OCR ▷ M1

Octal

Octal used to be a very popular method of displaying the binary contents of a computer, but hexadecimal is now more popular.

The octal number system uses eight digits that are 0,1,2,3,4,5,6,7. Each digit is worth eight times a similar digit to its immediate right. To translate an octal number into denary we can place the digits in columns that are labelled with their values:

64	8	1
1	3	4

The octal number 134 would represent:
$1 \times 64 + 3 \times 8 + 4 \times 1 = 64 + 24 + 4 = 92$.

Translating binary to octal

Divide the binary number into groups of three digits (starting from the rightmost digit). You now convert each group of three digits into a single octal digit.

In order to convert 111110010111
divide the number into groups of three giving 111 | 110 | 010 | 111
the octal number becomes 7   6   2   7

To translate from octal to binary you simply reverse the process. To translate the octal value 234 we convert each octal digit into three bits:

   2   3   4
010 011 100

giving 010011100 (or 10011100).

Translating denary to octal

To translate a denary number to octal you should do the following:

1 Write down the column headings, starting with the right-hand column. You continue to add columns until you get to the column that has a value greater than the denary number.
2 You place a 0 in this column.
3 You now process each column from left to right. Divide the denary number by the column heading. The result is placed in the column and the remainder becomes the denary number still to be translated.

Take as an example the denary value 321. We write down the column headings, starting with 1, until we get to a number greater than 321. In this case it is 512.

You can avoid converting directly from denary to octal by translating first to binary and then translating the binary value to octal.

	512	64	8	1
Place a 0 in the first column	0			
Divide 321 by 64 = 5 remainder 1				
Place 5 in column, remaining value is 1	0	5		
Divide 1 by 8 = 0 remainder 1				
Place 0 in column, remaining value is 1	0	5	0	
Divide 1 by 1 = 1 remainder 0				
Place 1 in column	0	5	0	1

The required octal value is 0501 (or 501).

> **KEY POINT**
>
> Like hexadecimal, octal is a convenient method of entering and displaying values that are stored in the computer in binary.

Binary arithmetic

AQA	A2
OCR	M1

Binary addition

Binary addition is performed using the same rules as for denary arithmetic. When the total of a column consists of more than one digit then the first digit is carried into the next column to the left. An example is 110 + 111.

Total the rightmost column. The result of 0 + 1 is 1.

```
  1 1 0
  1 1 1 +
  ─────
      1
```

Total the next column. The result of 1 + 1 is 10 so the result is 0 and we carry 1:

```
  1 1 0
  1 ₁1 1 +
  ─────
    0 1
```

Total the next column. The result of 1 + 1 + 1 is 11. The result is 1 and we carry the 1:

```
  1  1  0
 ₁1  1  1 +
  1  0  1
```

Total the next column. The result of 0 + 0 + 1 is 1:

```
  1  1  0
  1  1  1 +
1 1  0  1
```

Binary subtraction

Binary subtraction is performed using the same rules as denary subtraction. When the result of a subtraction is negative a 10 is borrowed from the next column. The important difference is that 10 in binary has a value of 2 in denary. An example is 110 – 101.

Subtract 1 from 0. The result –1 so we borrow 10 from the next column.
Subtract 1 from 10 giving 1:

```
  1  ¹⁰0
  0₁  1  –
      1
```

The one that was borrowed must now be subtracted from the next column.
Subtract this 1 from 1 giving 0:

```
  1  ¹⁰0
  0₁  1  –
  0   1
```

Binary multiplication

Binary multiplication is performed using the same rules as denary multiplication. As an example 110 x 101 would be calculated using long multiplication as follows.

```
     110
     101  x
     110
   110
   11110
```

Binary division

Binary division is performed using the same rules as denary division. As an example 10010/11 would be performed using long division as follows:

```
        110
   11 |10010
       011
      0011
        11
       000
```

> Binary arithmetic uses the same rules as denary arithmetic, but remember that each column has a value twice that of its neighbour.
>
> **KEY POINT**

Progress check

1 Translate the denary number 375 into:
(a) binary
(b) hexadecimal
(c) octal.

2 Translate the binary number 011010110001 into:
(a) denary
(b) hexadecimal
(c) octal.

3 Translate the hexadecimal number 8E into:
(a) binary
(b) denary.

4 Perform the following binary calculations:
(a) 1011001 + 10101
(b) 1011001 − 10101
(c) 11001 x 101
(d) 11001 / 101.

4 (a) 1101110 (b) 1000100 (c) 1111101 (d) 101.
3 (a) 10001110 (b) 142.
2 (a) 1713 (b) 6B1 (c) 3261.
1 (a) 101110111 (b) 177 (c) 567.

3.2 Coding of data

After studying this section you should be able to:

- *translate signed and unsigned integers*
- *translate binary coded decimal representation*
- *translate floating point representation*
- *translate character codes*
- *describe methods for storing sound and images*

LEARNING SUMMARY

Unsigned integer

AQA	M1
EDEXCEL	M2
OCR	M1
WJEC	CP1, CP2

An unsigned integer is stored as a pure binary number. It allows the storage of positive integers only. If we consider an unsigned integer which is stored as eight bits, the smallest value that can be stored is 00000000 which represents 0 and the largest value that can be stored is 11111111 which represents 255.

> **KEY POINT**
>
> Unsigned integers are used for positive integers only.

Signed integer

AQA	A2
EDEXCEL	M2
OCR	A2
WJEC	CP1, CP2

You can tell whether the number is positive or negative from the first bit. This is true for both sign and magnitude and twos complement format.

Sign and magnitude

When the sign and magnitude format is used, the leftmost digit is not part of the value but is used to represent the sign of the number. If the leftmost digit is a 0 then the sign is +, and if the leftmost digit is 1 the sign is –. Let us consider the numbers +5 and –5 stored in eight binary digits using sign and magnitude. They would be stored as follows:

+5 = 00000101
–5 = 10000101

Twos complement

Another method of storing negative numbers is called twos complement. The problem with sign and magnitude is that arithmetic with negative numbers is difficult. If you were to add +5 and –5 the result would be –10. If the numbers are stored in twos complement format then the result would be 0.

In order to translate a negative denary number to twos complement you need to perform the following steps:

1 Find the binary value of the denary number ignoring the minus sign.
2 Add 0s to the left of the value (you will always be asked to store the twos complement representation in a set number of bits).
3 Change all the 1s to 0s and all the 0s to 1s (we call this 'flipping the bits').
4 Add 1 to the result.

To translate –5 to twos complement format in 8 bits we would perform the following:

1 Translate 5 to binary   101
2 Add 0s to the left making the number 8 bits long 101 $\Rightarrow$ 00000101
3 Flip the bits   00000101 $\Rightarrow$ 11111010
4 Add 1   11111010 + 1 = 11111011

To translate a twos complement number to denary you must first check the leftmost bit to decide whether it is 0 (+) or 1 (–). If it is 0 (+) you can simply convert the binary number to denary. If it is 1 (–) you can discover the positive value by flipping the bits and adding 1.

To translate 1111101 to denary we must:

1 Flip the bits   11111011 $\Rightarrow$ 00000100
2 Add 1   00000100 + 1 = 00000101

This gives the denary value 5 so the twos complement number represents the value –5.

> Positive integers are stored in the same manner as sign and magnitude, only the negative values are stored differently.

	K E Y P O I N T
To change the sign of a twos complement number you flip the bits and add 1. This is true whether the number is positive or negative.	

Binary coded decimal (BCD)

AQA	M1
EDEXCEL	M2
OCR	M1
WJEC	CP1, CP2

> BCD is easy to convert from character format (see below) but arithmetic is more complex.

This method codes each denary digit into an unsigned binary value that is stored in four bits. To convert the denary value 274 into BCD each digit is encoded separately:

2 becomes 0010, 7 becomes 0111, 4 becomes 0100

2	7	4
0010	0111	0100

So the result is 001001110100.

Floating point

AQA	A2
EDEXCEL	M2
OCR	A2
WJEC	CP1, CP2

> Floating point allows a large range of values to be stored, but they are not stored precisely.

Floating point is the format used to store numbers that have a decimal point. Floating point format has two parts: the mantissa and the exponent. Many calculators use this format to display numbers that are too large or too small to be displayed using the normal format. The number 1 572 000 000 might be displayed on a calculator as 1.572 E9 which represents 1.572×10^9, where 1.572 is the **mantissa** and 9 is the **exponent**. The exponent is an instruction to move the decimal point. This allows the calculator to display a much larger range of numbers.

The computer stores binary fractions in the same way. A fixed number of bits are allocated to the mantissa and the exponent, for example ten bits might be used for the mantissa and six for the exponent. The mantissa will store the binary value and the exponent will state how many places to move the binary point. The binary point is always placed after the first bit in the mantissa, so 0110100000 would represent 0.1101. This is called **normalised** form. In this manner the value 3.25 might be stored as:

Mantissa	Exponent
0.110100000	000010

Positive exponents cause the point to move to the right (or make the number bigger). Negative exponents cause the point to move to the left (or make the number smaller).

The exponent has the value 2 so the binary point must be moved two places to the right. This gives us the value 11.01 which translates to 3.25 in decimal format.

> The size of the mantissa determines the precision of the value and the size of the exponent determines the range of values that can be stored.

Character representation

AQA	M1
EDEXCEL	M2
OCR	M1
WJEC	CP1, CP2

Whenever a key is pressed on a keyboard the character entered has to be stored in a binary code. The most common coding system is known as ASCII. The standard ASCII coding system uses seven bits to store one character, but there is now an extended ASCII coding system that uses eight bits. The ASCII codes for each character (excluding the extended character set) are shown in the following table.

Character	ASCII	Character	ASCII	Character	ASCII	Character	ASCII
space	00100000	8	00111000	P	01010000	h	01101000
!	00100001	9	00111001	Q	01010001	i	01101001
"	00100010	:	00111010	R	01010010	j	01101010
#	00100011	;	00111011	S	01010011	k	01101011
$	00100100	<	00111100	T	01010100	l	01101100
%	00100101	=	00111101	U	01010101	m	01101101
&	00100110	>	00111110	V	01010110	n	01101110
'	00100111	?	00111111	W	01010111	o	01101111
(	00101000	@	01000000	X	01011000	p	01110000
)	00101001	A	01000001	Y	01011001	q	01110001
*	00101010	B	01000010	Z	01011010	r	01110010
+	00101011	C	01000011	[	01011011	s	01110011
,	00101100	D	01000100	\	01011100	t	01110100
-	00101101	E	01000101	]	01011101	u	01110101
.	00101110	F	01000110	^	01011110	v	01110110
/	00101111	G	01000111	_	01011111	w	01110111
0	00110000	H	01001000	`	01100000	x	01111000
1	00110001	I	01001001	a	01100001	y	01111001
2	00110010	J	01001010	b	01100010	z	01111010
3	00110011	K	01001011	c	01100011	{	01111011
4	00110100	L	01001100	d	01100100			01111100
5	00110101	M	01001101	e	01100101	}	01111101
6	00110110	N	01001110	f	01100110	~	01111110
7	00110111	O	01001111	g	01100111	del	01111111

You will not be expected to memorise the ASCII table but you should be able to use it to translate characters into a binary code.

Another coding system that is used on some mainframe computers is EBCDIC. This also uses an 8 bit code. A new coding system is UNICODE. This uses a 16 bit code and is capable of representing 65 536 different characters. The UNICODE is capable of storing characters in every language in use today.

> This format is used to represent characters when they are entered on a keyboard or output to a screen or printer. It is also used when storing text within a computer system.

Sound representation

AQA	M1
EDEXCEL	M1
OCR	M1
WJEC	CP2

Sound is transmitted in the form of waves. This is known as an analogue signal and it is usually transmitted in the form of varying voltages or currents. Before sound can be stored in a digital computer it has to be converted to digital form. This conversion is done by an **analogue-to-digital converter** that samples the analogue signal regularly (see Figure 7). Each time the signal is sampled the analogue-to-digital converter measures the height of the wave and outputs the measurement as a binary value. This gives a sequence of numbers that can be stored.

When the sound is recreated the software can sample ahead and smooth out any inconsistencies in the data. In this way it can remove faults in the data caused by, for example, a scratch on a CD.

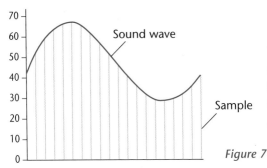

Figure 7

The wave can be stored as a series of samples. This wave might be stored as 42, 52, 59, 63, 65, 67, 66, 62, 57, 52, 46, 41, 38, 32, 29, 28, 30, 32, 36, 41

The sound wave can be recreated from the digital data by a digital-to-analogue converter.

> **KEY POINT**
> Once sound is in digital form it can be stored on any digital storage device such as magnetic disk or tape as well as CD.

Image representation

AQA	M1
EDEXCEL	M1
OCR	M1
WJEC	CP2

Images can be stored in various formats, but the simplest method is known as bitmap graphics. An image is displayed on a computer screen as a series of dots (or pixels) and each pixel is represented by a value in the computer.

In the case of a black and white image a pixel is represented by a single bit. The value 1 may represent white and 0 may represent black (or vice versa). Figure 8 shows an example of a black and white image. In order to represent a coloured image each pixel will be represented by a value that will specify the colour of the pixel.

Another method is known as vector graphics. An image is stored as a set of instructions that describe the constituent parts. These instructions can be used to recreate the image. The amount of storage used is normally much less than a bitmap and is dependent on the complexity of the image.

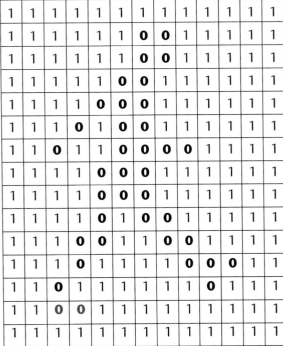

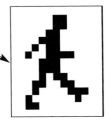

Figure 8 A bitmapped black and white image

Progress check

1 What is the value being stored in the 8 bit value 11111110 if the format of the data is (a) Unsigned binary, (b) Sign and magnitude, (c) Twos complement?

2 What would the 16 bit pattern 0110100000000011 represent if it holds a floating point value in the form of a 10 bit mantissa followed by a 6 bit exponent?

3 If the following bits represent characters using the ASCII character set, what message is represented?
00111110 01010001 01011010 01011101 01011011

4 What is the function of a digital-to-analogue converter?

Sample questions and model answers

1

(a) Translate the denary value 47 into

   (i) Binary

(a)(i)

64	32	16	8	4	2	1
0	1	0	1	1	1	1

   (ii) Hexadecimal.

(a)(ii) Dividing the binary number into groups of four bits we get

     0010   1111

     This translates to 2F in hexadecimal.

(b) How would the value −47 be stored in 8 bits in

   (i) Sign and magnitude format?

(b)(i) The value +47 would be stored as   00101111

     Thus, the value −47 would be stored as 10101111

   (ii) Twos complement format?

(b)(ii) The value +47 would be stored as   00101111

     Flipping the bits gives   11010000

                                 1 +

                             11010001

     So −47 would be represented as   11010001

2

A floating point format consists of a 10 bit mantissa followed by a 6 bit exponent. Both the mantissa and the exponent use twos complement format. What is the decimal value of 0110111000000100 if it contains this format?

Mantissa   Exponent

0110111000   000100

The value of the mantissa is 0.110111

The value of the exponent is 4 so we must move the binary point 4 places to the right. This gives the value 1101.11

8	4	2	1	½	¼
1	1	0	1	1	1

The decimal value is 8 + 4 + 1 + ½ + ¼ = 13.75.

Practice examination questions

1 The binary pattern 1011 1010 0011 can be interpreted in a number of different ways.
   (a) State its hexadecimal representation. [1]
   (b) State its value in denary if it represents a twos complement floating point number with an 8 bit mantissa followed by a 4 bit exponent. [3]

   AEB

2 (a) In Computer A, positive or negative integers are represented by the use of twos complementation, using 8 bits.
      (i) Show how the number $+30_{10}$ is represented. [1]
      (ii) Show how the number -30_{10} is represented. [1]
   (b) In Computer B, positive or negative integers are represented by the use of 1 sign bit and 7 magnitude bits. The sign bit is the most significant bit, and is **set to 1** to represent negative and **set to 0** for zero or positive. Show how the number –3010 is represented in this case. [1]
   (c) (i) Convert the number 2910 into hexadecimal. [1]
      (ii) Binary numbers used by computers are often converted into hexadecimal numbers for the benefit of human programmers. Describe the advantage of hexadecimal over binary for the programmer. [1]
      (iii) These binary numbers could instead be converted into denary (base 10). Describe the advantage of hexadecimal over denary. [1]

   WJEC

3 (a) How would the decimal number 1025 be stored in a 16 bit register? [2]
   (b) Using hexadecimal as a shorthand notation, how would you write your binary number? [2]
   (c) The hexadecimal character code for the digit 1 is 31. State how 1025 would be represented using this coding system. [2]

   NEAB 1998, CPO2

Chapter 4

System software

The following topics are covered in this chapter:

- *Operating systems*
- *Systems programs*
- *Translation programs*

4.1 Operating systems

After studying this section you should be able to:

- *describe the purpose of an operating system*
- *understand the common features of operating systems*

Purpose of an operating system

AQA	M1, M2
EDEXCEL	M1
OCR	M1
WJEC	CP2

An operating system is a set of computer programs that controls the operation of the computer system. It provides an environment that makes it easy for the user to access the various parts of the computer system and manages the memory, storage devices and the input/output devices. It is often said that the operating system provides a virtual machine.

User interfaces

AQA	M1, M2
EDEXCEL	M1
OCR	M1
WJEC	CP2

The user interface is the view a user has of the operating system. The most popular form of user interface is currently the WIMP (Windows Icons Mouse Pointer) environment. It should be appreciated that an operating system may have a range of user interfaces to be used as appropriate.

Although PCs running Microsoft Windows normally have a single interface, this is not the case with other operating systems. Unix offers a range of interfaces, some of which are WIMP environments.

Graphical user interface (GUI)

A graphical user interface displays information in a pictorial manner. The most common type of GUI is known as the WIMP interface. This interface displays windows that contain icons (small pictures). The user interacts with the interface via a pointer (cursor) that is moved with a mouse (or other similar device). By moving the pointer over an icon and selecting it (usually by pressing one of the buttons on the mouse) it is possible to instruct the computer. There is also a menu system that allows the user to select various options.

The advantages of this type of interface are:

- It should be intuitive so that it is easy to use
- A beginner does not have to learn a set of instructions to operate the machine.

The disadvantages are:

- It uses a lot of processing power
- It requires a good graphical display
- It uses a lot of memory and disk space
- It can be slow for experienced users.

Modern PCs have enormous processing power compared with previous computer systems but most of that power is used to maintain the Microsoft Windows operating system.

Command line interface (CLI)

A command line interface requires the user to enter a typed instruction to the operating system. These interfaces can be very efficient when the user is skilled but the beginner often finds it difficult to get started. A really skilled operator may manage to achieve several tasks from one instruction. An example of such a command is:

COPY C:\MYFILE.DOC A:\MYFILE.DOC

This might copy the file MYFILE.DOC from the hard drive to the floppy drive.

Job control language (JCL)

A batch operating system is required to execute a series of batch jobs (a job is a name given to a batch update that might involve several programs) without human intervention. In order to do this, each job is entered into the system along with a series of commands written in JCL.

> **KEY POINT**
>
> The user interface needs to be appropriate for the purpose, so operating systems often provide a range of user interfaces.

Resource management

AQA	M1, M2
EDEXCEL	M1
OCR	M1
WJEC	CP2

Resource management is probably the most important feature of an operating system. If this is done well it improves the overall performance of the computer system.

When a program is being executed it is known as a process. There are often conflicts in a computer system when a resource (such as the printer) is requested by more than one process. The operating system has to manage requests for resources and allocate the resources in an orderly manner. It will allocate memory and control the execution of programs.

One method of improving the effectiveness of a computer system is to execute more than one program at the same time. This is known as multiprogramming and gives rise to a number of computer terms:

- Single-user – an operating system designed for a single user
- Multi-user – an operating system that allows several users access concurrently (this is also known as multi-access)
- Timeslicing – the operating system allocates small slices of time to each task
- Single-tasking – executing one task at a time
- Multitasking – executing more than one task concurrently.

File management

AQA	M1, M2
EDEXCEL	M1
OCR	M1
WJEC	CP2

The operating system will control the transfer of data to and from the storage devices. In order to make this easier for the user the operating system will organise the files on the storage device. Magnetic disks often hold a large number of files and it can be quite difficult to find a particular file. To enable the user to organise the files, a hierarchical directory structure is normally implemented. An example is illustrated in Figure 9.

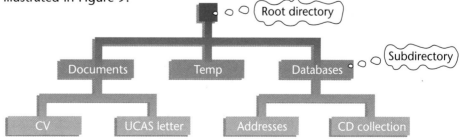

Figure 9

The top-level directory is known as the **root directory**. The root directory can contain either file names or subdirectories. It is normal practice to organise similar files within a subdirectory. Although Figure 9 shows only one level of subdirectory it is possible to have as many levels as you wish. To access a file it is necessary to state the position of the file in the directory structure as well as the name of the file (known as the **pathname**). To specify the file named 'Addresses' the pathname might be

\Databases\Addresses

Different operating systems use different naming conventions but they will normally provide a hierarchical directory structure. Sometimes a directory is called a folder.

> The file system is a flexible system provided to enable the user to organise the files in such a way that they are easy to find.

File extensions

File names will often contain a three-character extension, for example:

CV.DOC

Extension

The extension is used to describe the type of data to be stored in the file. Examples of file extensions are:

- DOC – a word processing document
- TXT – a text file with no formatting
- PAS – a Pascal program
- EXE – an executable program
- CPP – a C++ program
- DLL – a dynamic link library.

The operating system can use this information to display an appropriate icon in a WIMP environment and it can use the extension to select an appropriate program to access the file.

> File extensions indicate to the operating system the type of data to be found in a file.

Types of operating system

AQA	M1, M2
EDEXCEL	M1
OCR	M1
WJEC	CP2

There are a number of different types of operating system that control different environments.

Batch

> Batch processing has to be able to execute long processes efficiently. The system has a large number of updates to perform and it has to execute these as quickly as possible.

This environment is suitable for computer systems that are running processes that may take some time to complete. The processes are allowed to continue to completion without intervention from the user. Examples might be a payroll program, and banking systems that update a day's trading overnight.

Interactive

An interactive environment will have one or more users performing tasks directly

An interactive system has to respond immediately to a user even at the expense of efficiency elsewhere. People become very impatient if they have to wait for even a split second.

through a workstation. It must provide a user interface that allows good communication with the user. The operating system must respond quickly to the user. This does not mean that the system will perform tasks immediately, but it should keep the user informed of progress.

Real-time

Real-time systems have to respond to users immediately and they also have to perform updates rapidly. The updates are normally small changes to data files rather than the large updates performed in batch processing.

A real-time environment will require that data received by the system are processed immediately so that it maintains a completely up-to-date environment. Real-time systems also have to provide sophisticated protection systems so that it is not possible for different users to update the same data at the same time. An example of this problem is the real-time booking system when two users could attempt to book the same seat on a plane. Typical uses of a real-time system might be an air traffic control system or a real-time banking environment.

Network

The whole issue of networking is dealt with in Chapter 5.

A network operating system must be able to provide an environment over a number of computers that are connected together in a computer network. It will enable access to resources on other computers and may even use the combined computing power of several computers to solve a problem.

Different types of operating system will attempt to make different parts of their operation as efficient as possible. **KEY POINT**

Progress check

This question introduces another problem with command line interfaces, namely that instructions can be mistyped with possibly disastrous consequences.

1 It is possible to mistype a command in a command line interface and this can cause unexpected results, for example the user may wish to delete the file TABLEFILE. Instead of entering
    DEL TABLEFILE
the user enters
    DEL TABBEFILE
If TABBEFILE exists it will be deleted by mistake.

(a) Explain why such errors are unlikely to occur when using a WIMP environment.
(b) Give **one** additional advantage of a WIMP environment.
(c) Give **one** advantage of a command line interface.

1 (a) In a WIMP environment the user will be presented with an icon to represent the file and it is unlikely that the user will select the wrong icon by mistake.
(b) An advantage of a WIMP environment is that it is easier for the beginner as he/she does not have to learn a set of commands.
(c) An advantage of the command line interface is that it can be faster to enter commands when the user is skilled.

4.2 Systems programs

After studying this section you should be able to:

- *explain what a systems program is*
- *describe various systems programs*
- *explain the term library program*
- *explain the term utility program*

The need for systems programs

AQA	M1
EDEXCEL	M2
OCR	M1
WJEC	CP2

The term 'systems programs' should not be confused with utility programs. It is convenient to write an operating system as a series of systems programs. A large number of these will be utility programs but some will be essential parts of the operating system.

An operating system needs to be able to perform a large number of tasks and it would be impossible to encompass all of these tasks into one large program. As a result an operating system will consist of a large number of small programs that will be called into use as required. These separate programs are called systems programs. Examples of systems programs are:

- Spooler – to deal with the printer queue
- I/O drivers to deal with the various different devices that can be connected to the system
- Disk managers – to organise the disk and/or check it for errors
- Virus checkers – to check for and remove viruses
- Utility programs – see below
- Monitor programs – to monitor the performance of the system
- Networking programs – to allow the system to be used on a network.

Library program

AQA	M1
EDEXCEL	M2
OCR	M1
WJEC	CP2

A library program is a program that is stored on a disk in a special type of file (called a library) and is available to all users of the system. The library program may be a systems program or any other task that is useful to users of the system. Some libraries contain library routines that can be incorporated into users programs. A library is simply a convenient method of storing a large number of small programs. The alternative would be to have a large number of small files.

Utility program

AQA	M1
EDEXCEL	M2
OCR	M1
WJEC	CP2

Any systems program that is not essential for the execution of the user's programs can be called a utility program.

A systems program that performs a specific task for the user of the system may be called a utility program. The utility programs will normally be stored in a library and so they will be library programs. Most of these tasks refer to data that are stored in files; examples are:

- Disk formatter – prepares a new disk for use
- Disk copier – to copy data from one disk to another
- Sort – to sort data into sequence
- Editor – to allow the creation and modification of text files
- Data compression – to reduce the amount of space taken up by a file.

> An operating system will consist of a large number of small programs that work together to provide a virtual machine. Most of these programs are totally hidden from the user of the computer system.
>

Progress check

Any of the programs that will normally be provided with an operating system can be regarded as systems programs. There are, therefore, many possible answers to this question.

1 Describe five systems programs that might be found in a typical operating system.

1 Spooler – a program that will deal with the various requests to use the printer
File manager – a program to manage the file system
Virus checker – a program to check for and remove viruses
Editor – a program to allow text files to be entered and modified
Disk formatter – a program to prepare a new disk for use on the system.

4.3 Translation programs

After studying this section you should be able to:

- *state the need for translation programs*
- *describe different translation programs*

The need for translation programs

AQA	M1
EDEXCEL	M2
OCR	M1
WJEC	CP1, CP2

A more detailed description of the various languages is to be found in Chapter 8.

A computer program is a set of instructions that we wish the computer to perform. Machine code is a set of binary codes that the computer understands and executes. We find it very difficult to write programs in machine code so we have invented a number of other languages that are easier for us to use. Assembly code is a language that has one instruction for each machine code instruction. There are high-level languages that have instructions that need to be converted into a number of machine code instructions. The program that converts one language into the other is called a translation program.

Assembler

AQA	M1
EDEXCEL	M2
OCR	M1
WJEC	CP1, CP2

The assembler converts assembly code instructions into machine code. One assembly code instruction produces one machine code instruction so this is a comparatively simple process. Assembly code is used when it is essential to write efficient programs or when it is not possible to make the computer perform the task using any other language.

Compiler

AQA	M1
EDEXCEL	M2
OCR	M1
WJEC	CP1, CP2

A compiler is used to convert a high-level programming language into machine code. One high-level language instruction produces several machine code instructions so this is a more complex program than the assembler. A high-level language will have specific features to solve particular problems rather than being limited by the machine code instructions available. These languages make it much easier to program the computer but the compilers do not produce very efficient machine code so they will take up more memory and will execute more slowly.

Interpreter

AQA	M1
EDEXCEL	M2
OCR	M1
WJEC	CP1, CP2

An interpreter will also convert a high-level program but it does not produce a machine code version. Instead of generating the machine code for use later it executes the program directly. When the interpreter executes a program it converts each instruction one at a time. This allows the translation process to be quicker but the program will execute very slowly. As the interpreter is always in control it is possible to control the way the program runs and so this is ideal for a development environment where the programmer is writing and testing a program. When an interpreter is used it is often possible to stop the program at various points and inspect the state of the program.

> An interpreter is used when developing a program owing to its ability to control the execution of the program. A compiler or assembler will be used to produce an executable version when the program is fully tested and working.

KEY POINT

Progress check

1 A programmer is developing a program in a high-level language and has the choice of an interpreter or a compiler to translate the program. Give:
   (a) **one** advantage of the compiler and
   (b) **one** advantage of the interpreter.

1 (a) The compiler has the advantage that the code produced will execute more efficiently.
(b) Either: the interpreter will translate the program more quickly than the compiler,
Or: the interpreter will provide debugging aids that will make it easier to develop the program.

Sample questions and model answers

1

Computer systems require both *application software* and *system software*.

(a) Distinguish between these two types of software. [2]

(a) Application software enables the user to do a job with the computer system. System software carries out tasks necessary for the operation of the computer.

There are many examples that could be given of an application or application package.

(b) Give **one** example of each. [2]

NEAB 1998, CP01

(b) An example of an application package is a word processor.
An example of a system program is a disk formatter.

Again, any sensible example will do.

2

Describe **two** of the operations carried out by an operating system in a Windows environment. [4]

OCR 1999, 6810

Typical operations that can be carried out are:

Always ensure that you give two different operations or you may not get all the marks.

(i) Copy files from one location to another, for example from hard disk to floppy disk.

(ii) Execute programs by double-clicking on their icons.

3

This question should be read carefully. Any utility that does not **update files** will get no marks.

Describe in detail **two** file utility routines used for the updating of files held on magnetic disk backing store. [4]

OCR 1998, 6810

A delete utility could be used to remove a file from the disk. It will be necessary to identify the file and the utility will remove the file and make the space available for another file.
An editor can be used to update a text file. The user identifies the file and is then able to add, delete or overwrite characters on the file.

Practice examination questions

1 Some computer systems use a **graphical user interface**, while others use a **command-driven interface**.
   (a) Briefly describe **one** characteristic feature of **each** of these two user interfaces. [2]
   (b) State **one** advantage of each, from the user's point of view. [2]
   NEAB 1999, CPO1

2 In a typical file operating system a file specification consists of a pathname, a file name, and a file extension. Explain with the aid of an example the purpose of these three components. [6]
   NICCEA

3 Many machines now offer a graphical user interface such as Windows.
   (a) Describe **two** features of such interfaces which are likely to be helpful to a non-technically minded user. [2]
   (b) Describe **three** disadvantages of this type of interface. [3]

4 Describe, with the aid of a diagram, a hierarchical directory structure. [3]
   NEAB 1998, CPO2

5 (a) Explain what is meant by a programming language. [2]
   (b) Distinguish between low-level and high-level programming languages. [2]
   (c) What must happen to the source code of a program before it can be executed, and why is this necessary? [2]
   NEAB 1999, CPO1

Chapter 5

Networking

The following topics are covered in this chapter:

- Data transmission
- Networks

5.1 Data transmission

After studying this section you should be able to:

- describe the basic protocols for transmitting binary data
- compare and contrast parallel and serial data transmission
- explain how asynchronous data transmission is effected
- explain the use of parity checks

LEARNING SUMMARY

Basic data transmission

AQA	M1
EDEXCEL	M1
OCR	M1
WJEC	CP2

When data are transmitted from one computer to another they travel along some medium (copper wire, optical fibre, as radio waves, infra-red) in the form of bits. For the purpose of this discussion we shall assume that the medium is a wire and the data are transmitted in the form of voltage changes. The sender will generate one voltage to represent 1 and a different voltage to represent 0. The sender has a clock and it transmits bits at regular intervals. At any point in time there will be a number of bits being carried along the wire so the voltage may be depicted as in Figure 10.

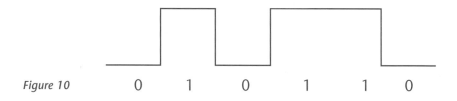

Figure 10   0   1   0   1   1   0

Baud

Do not confuse baud with bit rate. Baud is the rate that signals are sent.

The rate that the voltage changes is called the baud. In the simple case described above, if the voltage changes 10 times every second the baud is said to be 10.

Bit rate

The bit rate is the term given to the rate that bits are transmitted. In the simple case described above the bit rate is the same as the baud. If we could generate four voltages, instead of two, we could use each change in signal to represent two bits. Figure 11 depicts a case where data are transmitted using a signal that has four possible voltages.

Bit rate is a more useful measure than baud but the speed of a communication line is often measured in baud.

If the signals are transmitted 10 times a second, the baud rate is still 10 but 20 bits per second are being transmitted.

> The baud refers to the rate that signals are transmitted along a wire. The bit rate refers to the rate that bits are transmitted. The two may or may not be the same.

KEY POINT

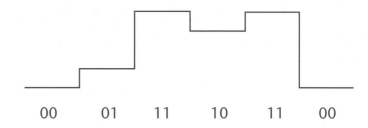

00　　01　　11　　10　　11　　00

Figure 11

Bandwidth

When a signal is transmitted along a wire (or any other medium) it is reluctant to travel as a square wave. Waves are naturally in the form of sine waves (also known as **analogue signals** – Figure 12).

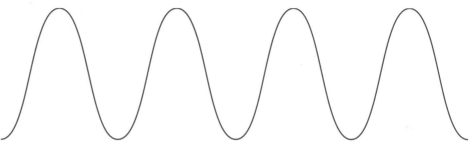

Figure 12

If you throw a pebble into a pond and watch the waves you will see that they are this shape. All media are capable of transmitting a set of waves that have a range of frequencies. The frequency of a wave is the rate at which the wave repeats itself (Figure 13).

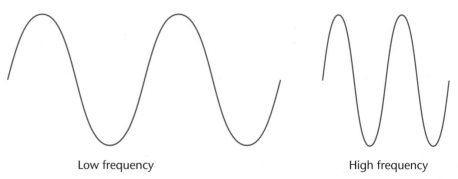

Low frequency　　　　　　　　　　　　　High frequency

Figure 13

This is a correct definition of bandwidth, but you will also come across the use of bandwidth to mean the amount of data that can be transmitted, for example a data bus may be said to have a greater bandwidth if it has more wires.

The range of frequencies that a medium can transmit is known as its **bandwidth**. The reason that this is important is that the wider the bandwidth, the more data that can be transmitted. A normal telephone wire has a very low bandwidth so it is not possible to transmit many data. An optical fibre has a very high bandwidth so it can transmit a very large amount of data.

> **KEY POINT**
> The higher the bandwidth the greater the amount of data that can be transmitted.

Parallel data transmission

AQA   M1
EDEXCEL M1
OCR   M1
WJEC   CP2

Data are normally transmitted in the form of bits that follow each other along a single wire. This is called serial data transmission. If we lay a number of wires alongside each other in parallel it is possible to transmit several bits at the same time (Figure 14).

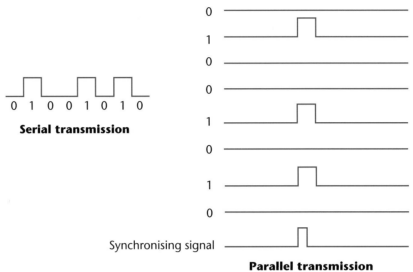

0 1 0 0 1 0 1 0
Serial transmission

0
1
0
0
1
0
1
0

Synchronising signal

Parallel transmission

Figure 14

Another wire contains a synchronising signal which is used to inform the receiving device that data should be present. Parallel transmission would appear to allow the data to be transmitted more quickly, but there is a problem. The data do not travel at the same speed down each wire. As a result the data bits tend to arrive at different times. This effect is known as **skew** (Figure 15).

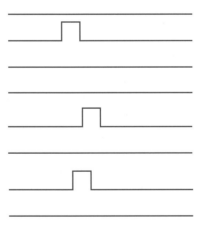

Figure 15 Skewed data

The parallel interface on the back of a PC is often called the printer interface or the printer port.

To prevent data being misread parallel transmission is only possible over short distances.

Parallel cables are more expensive because of the extra wires. They can be faster than serial but can only be used over short distances.

KEY POINT

Asynchronous data transmission

AQA	M1
EDEXCEL	M1
OCR	M1
WJEC	CP2

It is often necessary to be able to transmit data intermittently, for example a keyboard transmits characters to the computer when the user happens to press a key. This type of transmission is known as asynchronous data transmission. This can be performed one character at a time as follows. A character can be coded into 8 bits. Preceding the data bits there will be a start bit and following the data there will be a stop bit (Figure 16).

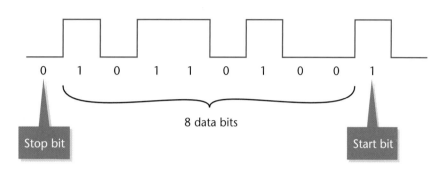

Figure 16

Two stop bits may be added to the back of the character. This is a historical idea that goes back to the days when electromechanical devices were used for data transmission. These devices needed the extra time that two stop bits gave them to ensure that everything had stopped moving before the next start bit arrived.

When no data are being sent the signal transmitted represents 0. This ensures that the first signal received is always a change from 0 to 1. This change in voltage can be used to start the clock of the receiving device. The receiver will then read the 8 data bits. The stop bit ensures that the next start bit will be recognised.

> **KEY POINT**
>
> In order to transmit a character asynchronously a start bit must be added to the beginning of the character and a stop bit must be added to the back of the character.

Transmission protocols

AQA	M1
EDEXCEL	M1
OCR	M1
WJEC	CP2

A protocol is simply another name for a rule. There are many rules that apply to data transmission and it is only possible to transmit data between devices that use the same protocol.

An example of a protocol is the signals that are sent to ensure that a device is ready to receive data when they arrive. In the case of parallel data transmission to a printer there will be additional control wires to allow the printer and the computer to communicate with each other. The computer will send a signal to the printer when it has data to send and the printer will respond with a signal to say that it is either busy or available to receive the data. This type of communication is called **handshaking**.

Another protocol is the rate that data are transmitted. In order for serial data transmission to be successful the receiving device must be set to receive data at the same bit rate as the sending device is sending the data.

Parity bits may be attached to data in order to check that the data received are correct. Taking the example of asynchronous data transfer described above, a parity bit might be added to the character as shown in Figure 17.

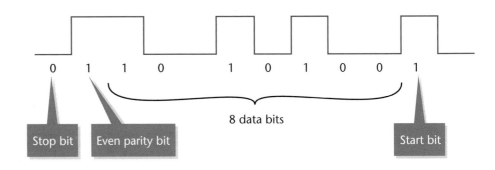

Figure 17

The parity bit is computed as follows:

1 Add up the 1s in the data bits.
2 If the total is an odd number the parity bit is 1, if it is even the parity bit is 0.

In this manner the total number of 1s in the data plus the parity bit should be an even number. If the receiver adds them up and the result is odd then it knows the data are in error.

It is also possible to use odd parity, in which case the total number of 1s in the data bits plus the parity bit should be an odd number.

> Parity bits do not provide complete protection against errors in data transmission but they are very popular nevertheless.

> **KEY POINT**
> A protocol is simply a set of rules. In the context of data transmission the protocol will specify such items as the baud rate, the method of encoding data, the method used to check for errors in transmission, and so on.

Progress check

1 Data are to be transmitted over a serial transmission line that is operating at 1000 bits per second. Data are encoded into 8 bit characters and transmitted using an asynchronous protocol that uses one start bit and one stop bit. What is the maximum data transfer rate in characters per second?

2 Data can be transmitted using either parallel or serial transmission. Give **one** advantage of serial transmission and **one** advantage of parallel transmission.

Parallel transmission is faster as several bits are transmitted at the same time.
2 Serial cable is cheaper than parallel cable as it has fewer wires.
second.
The line transmits 1000 bits per second therefore the character rate is 1000/10 = 100 characters per
1 One character requires 8 bits for the data + 1 start bit + 1 stop bit = 10 bits.

5.2 Networks

After studying this section you should be able to:

- define the terms LAN, WAN, Internet, intranet
- compare and contrast bus, ring and star topologies
- describe the purpose of a modem
- compare and contrast leased line and dial-up networking
- explain the addressing conventions of the Internet

Types of network

AQA	M1
EDEXCEL	M1
OCR	M1
WJEC	CP2

There are many different types of network but they generally break down into two distinct types, **local area networks** (or LANs) and **wide area networks** (or WANs). The main differences between these two networks can be described as follows:

LAN	WAN
Generally less than 1km in diameter	Generally more than 1km in diameter
Generally owned by one organisation	May be used by many organisations

These descriptions are very general and there are WANs that are owned and run by single organisations. The real difference between LANs and WANs is in their protocols.

Most networks use a client/server protocol where most users have a computer that acts as a client. In a client/server relationship the client asks the server to perform some task. Typical servers might be:

- File server – to store users data and/or programs
- Print server – to deal with printing
- Mail server – to provide e-mail
- Web server – to store web pages.

Network applications

AQA	M1
EDEXCEL	M1
OCR	M1
WJEC	CP2

You should always consider the possibility of using a network whenever you are asked to specify an application, but there are a number of specific applications that are only possible over a network.

Electronic mail

Electronic mail (or e-mail as it is commonly known) allows you to type messages on your computer and send them electronically through a network to other users. A user is identified by an e-mail address that is allocated to you when you start using the service. A computer is designated to be your e-mail server. This computer acts as a postbox and will store any messages you are sent and forward any messages that you wish to send. E-mail has the following advantages over normal mail:

- E-mails are transmitted immediately at high speed so they are received very quickly.
- You can transmit and receive directly from your desk.
- It is generally cheaper to send an e-mail.
- Messages can be sent securely as you have to know a password to access someone's e-mail.
- You can create address lists and send messages simultaneously to a number of people.

- You can attach files of information to an e-mail.

A related application is the electronic conference where people with the same interests can 'post' messages that everyone can read. This is like an electronic noticeboard.

Electronic funds transfer

Electronic funds transfer (EFT) allows the transfer of money directly from one bank account to another. A related application EFTPOS (electronic funds transfer at point of sale) allows payment by credit card and is creating a whole new industry known as e-commerce.

Video conferencing

With the aid of cameras it is possible to transmit live pictures and so to allow several people at different locations to hold a meeting over a network. This saves the time and cost of travelling to meetings.

Distributed systems

It is possible to organise computer systems that hold data at various locations and combine them to produce useful information. In this manner systems can use the combined power of several computers to produce results.

The most common protocol for distributed processing is the client/server protocol. The client computer requests a service from the server. The server processes the request and returns the results. On one network there may be many servers.

Internet

The Internet is a worldwide network of computers that can be used by anyone through an **Internet service provider (ISP)**. It consists of a large number of networks that are connected together using a common protocol (known as TCP/IP). All of the applications described previously can be obtained via the Internet and in addition there is the **World Wide Web**. The World Wide Web consists of a large number of web servers that each has a number of web pages. A web page is simply a document that can be viewed across the Internet using a program known as a **web browser**. In order to help you find information there are special servers known as **search engines**. You can ask the search engine to look for information on a particular subject and it will find some appropriate web pages.

Many organisations have now created local web pages that are viewable only on their local network. This type of system is known as an **intranet**.

LAN topologies

AQA	M1
EDEXCEL	M1
OCR	M1
WJEC	CP2

A topology is another name for the physical layout of a network. The common LAN topologies are star, bus and ring.

Star

A star network (Figure 18) has one computer at the centre and all the others connected directly to it. The advantages of a star network are:

- If one cable fails it affects only one computer.
- It is simple to isolate faults.
- It is easy to add and remove computers.

This is a very efficient network if all the services required are on one machine (for example a company that has its corporate database on a large mainframe).

- Different computers can transmit at different speeds.
- The system is more secure as messages are sent directly to the central computer and are not 'seen' by the other computers.

The disadvantages of a star network are:

- It uses a lot of cable and so it is expensive to install.

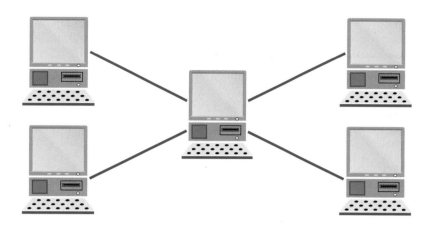

Figure 18

Bus

This topology is the cheapest in terms of cabling costs and also the most flexible as connections can easily be added to the network.

A bus network (Figure 19) uses a common cable to connect all the computers. The advantages of a bus network are:

- This is a very cheap means of networking as it uses the minimum of cable.
- It is very easy to add and remove computers.

The disadvantages of a bus network are:

- If the main cable fails the whole network goes down.
- It can take some time to isolate faults.
- The network degrades dramatically when highly loaded.

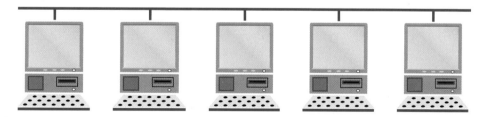

Figure 19

Ring

In a ring network (Figure 20) messages are passed around the ring in one direction only. The advantages of a ring network are:

Rings provide the fastest form of local area network.

- Collisions do not occur and so it is possible to calculate the maximum time that a message will take to get through.
- Very high transmission rates are possible.

The disadvantages of a ring network are:

- If the cable fails the whole network goes down.
- If any one computer fails it can bring the whole network down.

Figure 20

WAN connection

AQA	M1
EDEXCEL	M1
OCR	M1
WJEC	CP2

A WAN will normally use the telephone system to transmit data, but a normal telephone line will not carry digital signals: it will transmit only analogue signals within a very limited bandwidth. It is possible to convert digital signals to analogue and vice versa using a modem (Figure 21).

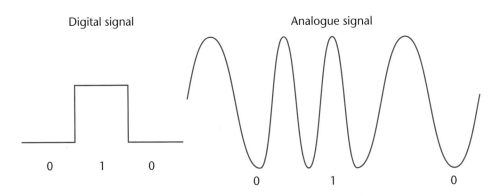

Digital signal   Analogue signal

0   1   0   0   1   0

Figure 21 *Signal converted by a simple FM modem*

New products are coming along all the time and much work is being done in mobile phone technology that is allowing users to have connection to their company's computer wherever they are.

As a result, British Telecom and other carriers offer a number of data services as well as the normal speech service. The options available are:

• Use a normal telephone line and a modem and dial up as required.
• Lease a digital line on a permanent basis.

Option 1 – use a normal line and a modem

This is the cheapest option if the line is not to be used very much. The main disadvantage is the speed. If a normal telephone line is used a modem must be employed and the modem will limit the rate at which data can be transmitted. The data can also be corrupted as speech lines are not guaranteed to be able to transmit data.

Option 2 – lease a digital line

A leased digital line is cheaper if the connection is going to be used for long periods. It is also possible to obtain guaranteed high-speed connections.

> A modem is required in order to transmit data over a telephone line. Modems are only able to transmit at limited speed, but it is possible to obtain special high-speed services from the telecommunication companies.
>
> **KEY POINT**

Internet addressing

AQA	M1
EDEXCEL	M1
OCR	M1
WJEC	CP2

An IP (Internet protocol) address uniquely identifies each computer that is connected to the Internet. An IP address is a set of four numbers such as 205.146.144.153. Each number is a value between 0 and 255. When a message is sent over the Internet, devices called routers inspect the address and pass the message on until it arrives at its destination. We find it difficult to remember these numbers so a set of domain names and URLs (universal resource locators) have been developed to make life easier for us. A domain name is the unique name for a computer on the Internet. A domain name ends with an extension that is either a country identifier or an international top-level domain. Examples are:

cocacola.com
bbc.co.uk

A computer with a domain name is popularly called a **site**. A site may have a number of servers associated with it. A server is a computer that provides a service to other computers on a network, for example a **web server** will hold web pages that can be viewed using a web browser. A URL is the name of a document that exists on the Internet and consists of a server name followed by the name and location of the document. For example:

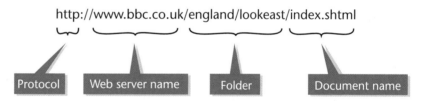

http://www.bbc.co.uk/england/lookeast/index.shtml

Protocol   Web server name   Folder   Document name

Figure 22

> A URL is the name that allows users to identify a device on the Internet. The URL has to be translated into the IP address that uniquely identifies the device.
>
> **KEY POINT**

Progress check

1 A school has decided to network its computers so that it can distribute information over a local intranet. The school also intends to connect the local network to the Internet.

(a) Describe three different topologies that could be used to network the computers.

(b) The various services are to be provided by servers. Briefly describe the services provided by:

(i) print server

(ii) Internet server

(iii) intranet server.

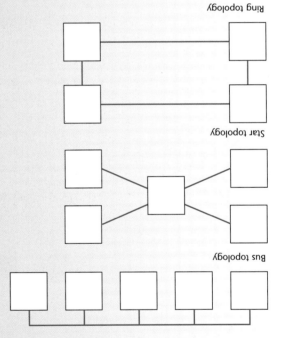

The following answers appear inverted (upside-down) on the page:

(iii) The intranet server will hold web pages that can be accessed by the users. Local information that the teachers wish to be available to the students will be placed here.

(ii) The Internet server will connect to the Internet through an Internet service provider. It will deal with requests for information from the World Wide Web. (An Internet server may incorporate a firewall that will limit the use of the Internet. A firewall can also protect the local network from hackers and viruses.)

(b) (i) A print server allows all the users of the network to share the printer. It will maintain a print queue and ensure that the printouts from different users do not get mixed up.

Ring topology

Star topology

Bus topology

1 (a) This part of the question can best be answered by drawing the various topologies.

Sample questions and model answers

1

A local newspaper group produces local papers for five different areas. The five local offices feed material into the central head office. There are two editions per week, on Tuesday and on Friday. Each has some pages devoted to special local news, with the rest of the material being common to all.

In one of the local offices there are two terminals devoted to advertisements and five for reporters, all running the same specialised software package. A reporter can type in a story, using basic word processing software, edit it, and, when ready, send it down a *leased line* to the head office.

(a) Why should a LAN be used within a local office?   [1]

> *(a) A LAN will allow resources, such as printers, to be shared.*
> *You can also save disk space by sharing the specialised*
> *software to be used by the reporters.*

This question looks substantial but it is really only asking you to show the examiner that you understand the use of LANs and WANs. Always apply your answer to the application described to make sure of full marks.

(b) Why should a WAN be used between offices?   [1]

> *(b) As the computers are spread over a wide area, a WAN will be*
> *required to communicate the reporters' work to head office.*

(c) Draw a diagram to show a suitable network topology for the LAN. Your diagram should include a suitable position for the file server and the direction of data flow.   [2]

AEB 1998, Paper 2

Any of the three standard LAN topologies can be drawn but be sure to mark the data flow.

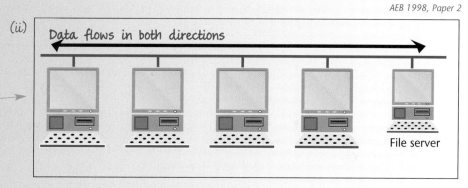

(ii) Data flows in both directions — File server

2

(a) Electronic mail (e-mail) is very popular.

   (i) Explain how you would prepare and send a message using e-mail.   [2]

You need to explain how you first prepare and then send an e-mail.

> *(a) (i) An editor or word processor is used to prepare the message.*
> *The e-mail address of the receiver is added and the message is*
> *sent.*

   (ii) Describe the role of an e-mail server.   [3]

There are 3 marks for this part so three features are required.

> *(ii) Each user has disk space for a mailbox that is identified by an*
> *e-mail address. The mailbox stores the user's messages.*
> *The server needs to be permanently online so the user can retrieve*
> *his/her messages. E-mail servers are linked by network so that they*
> *can forward messages to the receiver's e-mail server.*

(b) E-mail is now available on the Internet. How would a new user obtain an Internet e-mail address?   [1]

NEAB 1998, CPO2

> *(b) A new user would need to contact their e-mail provider. This may be a*
> *teacher at school, computer services at college, or alternatively a*
> *commercial organisation.*

Practice examination questions

1   On a local area network (LAN) the print server provides print spooling.
(a) What is the purpose of print spooling?   [2]
(b) What would be the effect if this feature did not exist?   [1]

NEAB 1997, CPO2

2   A local area network (LAN) is a collection of computers and peripherals linked by cables for the use of a single organisation or company. Most LANs are confined to a single office block or commercial site.

State **three** advantages of a LAN compared with the use of a collection of stand-alone microcomputers.   [3]

AEB 1996, Paper 1

3   The Internet is an international network of computer networks which provides access to computers located throughout the world. Many companies and educational establishments have placed information onto the Internet. Software such as web browsers and search engines facilitate access to this information.

(a) Give **two** reasons why an organisation places information onto the Internet.   [2]
(b) Give **two** examples of how the information available on the Internet might be used.   [2]

NEAB 1997, CPO2

4   For **each** of the following types of local area network (LAN), draw a diagram of a typical configuration.
(i) bus,   [1]
(ii) star,   [1]
(iii) ring   [1]

NEAB 1998, CPO2

5   The *Internet*, initially set up by the US Defence Department, now has many millions of users around the world. In the UK many schools and colleges have access to this web of computer networks.

Describe **one** advantage and **one** disadvantage of allowing young people unrestricted access to the Internet.   [2]

AEB 1997, Paper 1

Chapter 6

Information processing

The following topics are covered in this chapter:

- *Data entry*
- *Files*
- *File processing*

- *Databases*
- *Security*

6.1 Data entry

After studying this section you should be able to:

- *distinguish between data and information*
- *describe the various sources of data*
- *select appropriate methods of data entry*
- *explain how errors in the data can be detected and corrected*

LEARNING SUMMARY

Data and data gathering

AQA	M1, M2
EDEXCEL	M2
OCR	M1, M3
WJEC	CP2

A simple way to think of the difference between data and information is that a system will normally process data to produce information

Data consist of facts and figures that can be obtained from various sources. The purpose of an information processing system is to take in data and turn them into something useful that we call information. An example might be the national census. The data consist of millions of facts and figures about the population that have been recorded on paper and the information we need is how many people live in the different towns. The information system will calculate the totals and output them. Data can come either directly from the source or indirectly from other information systems, so the information from one system may be data for another.

Data may be gathered either manually or mechanically. Some of the common methods are:

There are other methods of data entry but these are the most common. The important point is to match the data entry method to the application.

- Keyboard entry – often from handwritten forms
- Optical character recognition – usually typed but can be handwritten
- Optical mark recognition – useful when the options are limited
- Barcodes – used on consumer products
- Data logging by other computers – such as palmtop devices
- Voice entry – security devices but may be more common in future
- Image capture by scanner or camera – useful when pictures are required.

> You need to select **appropriate** data entry methods for the application.
>
> KEY POINT

Data validation

AQA	M2
EDEXCEL	M2
OCR	M1, M3
WJEC	CP2

There are a number of checks that can be carried out to ensure that data are correct when they enter the system. Always consider what information is available to the system at the point of data entry before suggesting a validation method.

The examiner will be expecting you to show that you can select an appropriate method for the data being validated.

Character

Each fact or figure is normally called a **field** and the format of a field can be checked in various ways. If the field should contain a number it cannot have any alphabetic characters. In the same way a field containing a name cannot have numerical characters.

Format

Some fields have quite complex formats where numbers have to be in some places and characters in others, for example National Insurance code, postcode.

Length

Most fields have a maximum length and some have a minimum length.

Range

This normally applies to numerical fields. There may be an acceptable range of values.

Verification

This check can be applied when there is some means of comparing the data after entry with the correct version. Ideally the correct version is in the system on a file or database but this is often not available. In this case some systems will insist on the data being entered again to ensure they are correct (you may have been asked to do this with a password). A less efficient means of validating data is to ask the operator 'is this correct?' after all the data have been entered.

An automatic means of data verification is to add an extra digit (known as a check digit) to a field. This is normally applied to a code which is given by the computer, for example a bank account number, a stock code, etc. The computer calculates the check digit when the number is supplied. Every time the code is entered into the system the code is checked to ensure that the data are correct.

Control total

The supplier of the data is asked to total up some numerical field and enter this total with the rest of the data. This value can then be checked to ensure that the data covered by the total are correct. This control total may well be a useful total for manual processing as well: for example, the total number of packages in an order, the total value of an order.

Hash total

A hash total serves the same purpose as a control total only the total has no useful value except for checking purposes. An example might be to add up all the stock codes on an order.

Batch total

Often data are prepared off-line and transmitted to the system in batches. In this case batch totals may be used. A batch total applies to the whole batch, for example the total number of items in a batch.

> It is vital that you apply an appropriate validation check to data. Do not assume that you have access to the files or database unless the question tells you that this is the case.
>
> **KEY POINT**

Progress check

Describe appropriate validation checks for the following fields on an order form.

1 Name of customer.
2 Postcode.
3 Item number.
4 Quantity ordered.

1 The name field should be checked with a character check that will check that all the characters are alphabetic.
2 The postcode will require a format check. It will ensure that there are alphabetic characters and numerical characters in the right positions.
3 An item number can be checked with a range check as there will be only a certain range of numbers that have been allocated to valid item numbers.
4 The quantity field can be checked with a control total on the form. This will contain the sum of all the quantities ordered.

6.2 Files

After studying this section you should be able to:

- *describe the different types of file*
- *design record structures*
- *give appropriate storage devices for the different types of file*

LEARNING SUMMARY

File structure and types

AQA	M1, M2
EDEXCEL	M1, M2
OCR	M1
WJEC	CP2

A file is composed of a number of **records** and a record is composed of a number of fields. A field is one data item, for example a name or a price. A record consists of all the fields about one person or one item, for example an employee record (see Figure 23) or a stock item record.

Name of Field	
Name	Joe Harris
Street	17, The Lawns
Town	Surbiton
Postcode	SU2 3NB
Telephone Number	0171 344344
NI Number	XA 238466 A
Employee Number	172934
Department	Sales
Date Employed	12/04/1997

Figure 23 *An example of a personnel record*

> A record key must be unique so don't be tempted to suggest someone's name, as it is quite possible for two people to have the same name.

It is usually necessary to be able to identify a particular record, so one or more fields are selected as the **record key** (sometimes known as the **key field**). The important feature of this record key is that it must be unique, i.e. there must be no other records on the file with the same key. In Figure 22 (a personnel record) the record key would be the Employee Number as there will not be two employees with the same number.

On a disk, each file will have an entry in the directory. The directory will consist of the file's name and various other data items associated with it, for example the date and time the file was created. One item that may be stored is the file type that can indicate what type of data is stored. Another way of identifying the file type is by giving the filename an extension. Typical file types are:

- Binary – programs or binary data, .BIN
- Text – to store text, for example, .TXT
- Graphic – to store pictures, for example, .JPG, .GIF, .TIF, .BMP
- Sound – digitised sound, .WAV, .MP3
- Video – digitised video, .AVI
- Hypermedia – web pages, .HTML

Applications may use their own extensions, for example Microsoft Word uses .DOC.

Record types

AQA	M1, M2
EDEXCEL	M1, M2
OCR	M1
WJEC	CP2

Records can be fixed in size if all the records contain the same number of fields and all the fields are of a fixed size. Making a field a fixed size is often inconvenient as the length of names, addresses, descriptions and so on can be very variable. In this case variable length fields are required, leading to variable length records.

A more difficult problem is the situation where a variable number of fields is required. Consider the problem of storing a bank account. The customer will have some fixed fields, for example name, address, bank account number, but there will also be a variable number of transactions (deposits and/or withdrawals). This problem can be solved using a record that has a variable number of fields. A common solution is to use two record types: a record with all the fixed data and possibly a count of the number of associated transactions, followed by a variable number of transaction records.

Record Type	A/C Number	Name	Address	Tel. No
A	1926783	L. Rogers	19 High Street, Ongar	01134 191125

Record Type	Credit/Debit	Date	Description	Amount
B	C	01/05/2000	Counter Credit	250.00
B	D	03/05/2000	Cheque No 176534	26.34
B	D	04/05/2000	Cheque No 176535	134.28
B	C	12/05/2000	Counter Credit	50.00

Figure 24 An example of a set of records storing information about one bank account

> Variable length records can save space, but they are more difficult to process and make it more difficult to assess the size of a file in advance.

Serial file

AQA	M1, M2
EDEXCEL	M1, M2
OCR	M1
WJEC	CP2

A serial file contains data that are in no particular order. The records are stored in the order they are received and the file is always processed as a complete file. This type of file can be stored on tape or disk. A typical use for this type of file is a transaction file where the records are in the order in which they happen to have been entered into the system.

Sequential file

AQA	M1, M2
EDEXCEL	M1, M2
OCR	M1
WJEC	CP2

A sequential file is processed serially, i.e. it is not possible to jump straight to a particular record, but the records are stored in record key order. This type of file can be stored on tape or disk. Often the transactions will need to be sorted before they can be processed. In this case the sorted transactions will become a sequential file.

Indexed sequential file

EDEXCEL	M1, M2
OCR	M1
WJEC	CP2

An indexed sequential file cannot be stored on a tape. This type of file is in two parts: a sequential file and an index. The index contains the record keys and the disk addresses of the records in the sequential file. This allows direct access to any record without reading the rest of the file. An indexed sequential file will be the normal file type to suggest when a file needs to be direct access and also needs to be updated regularly.

Random file

AQA M1, M2

EDEXCEL M1, M2

OCR M1

WJEC CP2

A random file may also be called a hash file or a direct access file. It cannot be stored on tape. The file consists of a number of records that are numbered. The data are stored as follows. An algorithm is applied to the record key and this produces a record number. If there is space then the record is stored in this position. If there is not space then the record is placed in an overflow position. The overflow position is calculated using another algorithm. The simplest overflow algorithm is to try the following positions until a free space is found.

A random file is faster to access than an indexed sequential file. It is very effective as a lookup file (that is, a file that is not going to be updated). It is not so useful when the file is to be regularly updated as it can easily become disorganised.

> **KEY POINT**
> Indexed sequential files and random files can only be stored on disk, whereas serial files and sequential files can be stored on both disk and tape.

Progress check

There are many possible answers to this type of question. You need to ensure that the fields are relevant and not repeated, for example you are unlikely to get a mark for both age and date of birth.

Describe ten fields that might appear on a payroll file.

Name	The employee's name
Address	The employee's address
Postcode	The employee's postcode
Telephone	The employee's telephone number
NI Code	The employee's National Insurance number
ID	The employee's payroll number
Joined	The date the employee joined the company
Salary	The employee's annual salary
Grade	The employee's grade
Dept	The employee's department.
Tax Code	The employee's tax code

6.3 File processing

After studying this section you should be able to:

- describe methods of processing data stored in files
- explain when each method is appropriate

File processing options

AQA	M2
EDEXCEL	M2
OCR	M1
WJEC	CP1, CP2

In any information processing system there will be a master file that will contain the data that are to be kept about the system. In most systems the event that causes the master file to be altered is called a transaction. A transaction might be a customer of a bank withdrawing some money, a shop selling something, an order being placed, and so on. The transactions may be processed as they happen or they may be stored up on a transaction file to be processed later.

Update in place

AQA	M2
EDEXCEL	M2
OCR	M1
WJEC	CP1, CP2

If the master file is stored as an indexed sequential file or a random file it is possible to process the transactions as they occur, i.e. to update in place (sometimes known as, to update in-situ). This method is preferred when the **hit rate** (that is the proportion of the master file records that are to be updated) is low.

Figure 25

> Update in place can occur in other situations but it is essential in real-time applications.

Update in place is particularly suited to a system where the master file has to represent an up-to-date position, for example an airline booking system. Such systems are called real-time systems. When this processing method is used it is common practice to copy the transactions onto a log file as a backup.

> **KEY POINT**
>
> This would appear to be the ideal processing method but it can be quite slow if a large number of transactions are to be processed, so it is used only when no other method is available.

Sequential update

AQA	M2
EDEXCEL	M2
OCR	M1
WJEC	CP1, CP2

The other common method is to store the master file on a sequential file. If the transactions are placed on a sequential file in the same sequence as on the master file it is possible to process all the transactions in one pass through the files. The system reads the old master file and writes out a completely new master file. This method is preferred when the hit rate is high.

This process leaves us with an old master file and a new master file (Figure 26). The old master file is normally kept together with the transaction file as a backup. We call the old master file the father file and the new master file the son. This process

```
       ┌──────────────┐
       │ Transaction  │
       │    file      │
       └──────────────┘ ╲
                         ╲
                          ╲        ┌─────────────────┐        ┌──────────────┐
                           ──────▶ │  Update process │ ─────▶ │     New      │
                          ╱        │                 │        │   master     │
                         ╱         └─────────────────┘        │    file      │
       ┌──────────────┐ ╱                                     └──────────────┘
       │    Old       │╱
       │   master     │
       │    file      │
       └──────────────┘
```

Figure 26

normally continues until there are four levels of files, giving great grandfather, grandfather, father and son files. Common systems using this process are batch systems that gather together all the transactions for a period onto a transaction file, for example a payroll system. Other systems that use this process are online systems that collect transactions directly during the day and process them as a batch overnight. An example of this is a banking system that is only able to give you your balance at close of trading on the previous day.

> This method is very efficient when a large number of transactions are to be processed.
> **KEY POINT**

Progress check

A supermarket has point of sale (POS) terminals which have bar code readers so that they can record each sale as it occurs. Each POS terminal has access to a list of prices which is stored in its memory.

The store also has a minicomputer linked to the point of sale terminals which has a stock file containing details of the total stock of the supermarket. As items are sold, the stock file is updated and the transaction is logged on a log file. At the end of the day, a program reads the stock file and creates an order file which is then transmitted through a telephone link to the company's warehouse to obtain new stock for the following day.

> You need both to state and to justify an appropriate file access method. Look carefully at the use of the files before you make your decision, and then give your reasons for your choice.

1 State and justify an appropriate file access method for **each** of the following:
   (a) the stock file, (b) the log file, (c) the order file.

2 State **three** fields needed for:
   (a) a stock file record, (b) a log file record.

1 (a) As the stock file is to be accessed randomly by the point-of-sale terminals and in sequence when processing orders. Sequential organisation would be appropriate. Sequential organisation as indexed.
  (b) The log file will simply record transactions in no particular order so a serial file would be appropriate.
  (c) The order file will be created in the same sequence as the stock file so it will be a sequential file.
2 (a) Item Identifier or Item Number; Quantity in Stock; Reorder Quantity
  (b) Transaction Type; Item Identifier; Quantity Ordered/Sold
  (Although any three fields might get you the marks in this type of question, in this case you were asked for fields that are needed. Marks will only be given for fields that are essential.)

6.4 Databases

After studying this section you should be able to:

- give the advantages of a database approach
- explain how databases are indexed
- describe primary and secondary keys
- describe a query method

Database management systems

AQA	M2
EDEXCEL	M2
OCR	M2
WJEC	CP2

A database is a collection of related data. In the early days of information processing each application had its own master file. This led to a number of problems:

- Data duplication leading to wasted space and wasted time entering the data.
- Data inconsistency – updating an employee's address on the personnel file but not on the payroll file.
- It was not possible to share data among systems easily.

The database management system (DBMS) is a piece of software that is placed between the application and the file system. This allows the file system to be regarded as a related set of data. The main features of a database system are:

- The database stores data as a number of linked records.
- The database may have multiple indexes that allow data to be obtained using different record keys.
- The format of the data can be specified and the database system will check for consistent data.
- In a database system, data duplication will be minimised, so space is saved and data inconsistency is reduced.

Relational databases

AQA	M2
EDEXCEL	M2
OCR	M2
WJEC	CP2

The relational database stores its data in tables. An example might be a table of cars sold in a secondhand car showroom (Figure 27).

CARS TABLE				
Registration_No	Make	Type	Colour	Mileage
T656LKV	FORD	MONDEO	RED	29036
S143DVC	ROVER	400	BLUE	27735
T222LBD	FORD	MONDEO	BLUE	17824
T622AXS	NISSAN	PRIMERA	RED	22036
S774HLF	RENAULT	CLIO	YELLOW	21576
V476FFB	FORD	KA	GREY	10234

Figure 27

A row in a table is similar to a record in a file and a column is called an attribute. Each table will have a **primary key** that must be unique. This will be one or more of the attributes and is used to identify the row. In Figure 27 this would be the registration number. One table is often related to another table and to enable this one or more of the attributes may be designated **foreign keys**. If we consider a table of customers who have purchased the cars in Figure 27 we might have a table like that shown in Figure 28.

CUSTOMERS TABLE		
Customer-No	Customer-Name	Car
1346	F. JAMES	V476FFB
1347	K. LONG	S774HLF
1348	P. BARRETT	T656LKV
1349	A. BROWN	T622AXS
1350	H. BROWN	T222LBD
1351	B. JOHNSON	S143DVC

Figure 28

Notice that we have introduced a customer number to give a primary key to this table.

In this case the car registration number will be a foreign key.

Queries

AQA	M2
EDEXCEL	M2
OCR	M2
WJEC	CP2

Another feature of databases is the ability to ask questions of the database (called a query). In the case of a relational database the result of a query will be a table of values. An example of a query might be 'Select all the FORDs we have for sale'. There has to be a standard language for these queries and one method is **query by example**. In query by example you set conditions for the information you require by composing **relational expressions**. A relational expression is made up from column names, constant values and **relational operators**. An example might be:

    Make = 'FORD'

This will select all the rows where the column Make contains 'FORD'. Other relational operators are < (less than), > (greater than), <= (less than or equal to) and >= (greater than or equal to). Relational expressions can also be combined using AND, OR and NOT. It is possible to produce sophisticated queries that obtain data from more than one table, for example using the tables in Figures 27 and 28 we could select the customers who have purchased FORD cars as follows:

    CUSTOMERS.CAR = CARS.Registration_No AND CARS.Make = 'FORD'

> **KEY POINT**
> A database provides a range of features to handle the data that are held on magnetic disks and tapes. It separates the user from the physical storage of the data.

Progress check

What is meant by program-data independence in the context of a database management system?

A DBMS manages the file system and presents the program with a view of the data that is largely independent of the way the data are physically stored. It is, therefore, possible to change the way the data is stored without altering the programs. (The point of this question is that traditional programs access the files directly. Using a database the user is only aware of the data and their structure, not how they are stored.)

6.5 Security

After studying this section you should be able to:

- *define the terms security and integrity*
- *describe backing-up procedures*
- *explain how a system can recover from hardware or software failure*
- *state methods of preventing unauthorised access to online data*

Security procedures

AQA	M2
EDEXCEL	M1
OCR	M1
WJEC	CP2

Security is provided by introducing procedures and safeguards to ensure that data are not accidentally or maliciously corrupted. If data have not been corrupted they are said to have integrity.

> By backing-up data stored in a computer system regularly, data should never be lost no matter what happens to the computer system.

Backups

It is always possible to back up a file by creating another copy, typically on a magnetic tape. This version can be copied again so that three copies are in existence. One of these should be either taken to another location or placed in a fireproof safe as protection against fire.

> Encryption can be performed automatically and is a key method of providing a secure connection over the Internet.

Encryption

Data can be encrypted to appear garbled unless you know how to decrypt the data. This can prevent unauthorised access as the data will be meaningless.

Passwords

> By setting up a hierarchy of passwords different users can be given access to different files or programs.

Passwords can be applied to computer systems so users cannot access the data unless they know the password. Passwords can also be applied to individual files so that a hierarchy of passwords may exist. Passwords should be changed regularly in case they become generally known.

Virus guards

A virus is a small program that attaches itself to your files. When you use a file with a virus attached it loads itself into the memory of the computer. It is able to replicate itself so that every time a new file is used it attaches itself to that one as well. In this way it can gradually attach itself to all of your files. This would not be much of a problem (except that you are wasting disk space) but a virus may suddenly turn nasty and attack your computer by, for example, removing all the files from your hard drive. Fortunately there are programs that can detect viruses and guard against them (called virus checkers or virus guards). Updates for these programs appear regularly, as new viruses appear all the time.

Progress check

Explain how you can defend your files from the following risks:

1 Fire in the computer. **2** Hackers. **3** Virus attack. **4** Disgruntled ex-employees.

1 By taking regular backups and storing them away from the computer. 2 By using passwords to access the system.
3 A virus checker should be installed and updated regularly.
4 By changing the passwords regularly so that an ex-employee will not be able to access the system.

Sample questions and model answers

1

A hospital keeps its patients' records on a file (called the Patients File) which is stored on magnetic disk. For reasons of medical confidentiality, information about patients' illnesses is not included in the file.

When a patient arrives at the hospital his/her details are entered into the system. Before a patient number is allocated, the system checks to establish whether the patient is already on file from a previous visit to the hospital. A new patient is allocated a patient number.

The hospital also has a Wards File that contains details of which patients are currently in each ward. The Wards File contains the following:
Ward Identifier
Bed Number
Patient Number.
When a patient is admitted to a ward the Wards File is updated.

When the patient leaves the hospital the Wards File and the Patients File are updated accordingly.

The following diagram shows the processes and files involved.

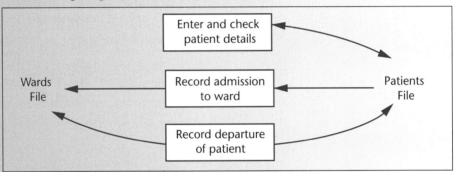

(a) State and justify, a suitable file organisation for **each** of the following:
(i) The Patients File [2]

(a) (i) The Patients File requires direct access and there is a requirement to add new patients, so an indexed sequential file organisation will be used.

(ii) The Wards File [2]

(ii) The Wards File will also need direct access but the wards themselves will not change so a random organisation will be used.

(b) When a patient arrives it is necessary to establish whether the patient is already on file. The patient will be asked for their name and address.
(i) State **two** other pieces of information, either of which could be used to help identify the patient. [2]

(b) (i) The patient's date of birth.
The patient's National Insurance number.

(ii) Give **five** additional fields that could be stored on the Patients File. [5]

(ii) The patient's telephone number
The patient's next of kin
The patient's doctor
The patient's doctor's telephone number
Date admitted to hospital.

NEAB 1999, CPO2

When a question has a long description of an application you will normally be asked to apply your answer to this situation, so read the question very carefully.

A number of answers are possible here, but the fields must not include name and address.

Again, a number of answers are possible but the fields must be in addition, so you will get no marks for repeating the fields given in (b).

Sample questions and model answers (continued)

2

Michael Deadlock has recently been made redundant after years of teaching Latin in a Sixth Form College in Tardyvale, a large and expanding market town. At 51 he feels too young to retire and has been exploring other work opportunities. In his research he has discovered that there appears to be a large demand for the hire of video films for viewing at home, and that the nearest video hire shop is in Tardyvale, some five miles from the large village in which he lives. Since there are a number of small shop premises available for rent locally, he has decided to investigate the possibilities of setting up a video hire shop in his village. A systems analyst friend (you) has offered to help him with any necessary research.

The first part of the investigation has proved positive. You and Michael have concluded that there is a demand for such a service. You have estimated that about 1000 people would use the service frequently, and another 2000 would use it occasionally. This information is sufficient to suggest to Michael that he should set up such a venture. He decides to go ahead with the project and is willing to invest some of his redundancy money in doing so. His initial stock consists of 4000 videos covering 800 different titles.

The business will need to hold information about its customers and the stock held.

(a) Suggest, with a reason, an appropriate piece of software for this purpose.   [2]

(a) A database package would be required. This would make it easy
     to manipulate the data.

(b) Suggest, with an example if appropriate, **four** essential fields which should be present in each of (i) the customer record, and (ii) the stock record, in each case giving a reason for their presence.   [16]

(b) (i)

Field	Reason
Customer Reference	To uniquely identify the customer
Customer Name	To identify the customer in the shop
Address	To send accounts, etc.
No. of Videos on Hire	To ensure that the maximum is not exceeded

The key point here is that the fields should be **essential**.

(ii)

Field	Reason
Video Code	To uniquely identify the video
Title	To identify the video in the shop
Date of Borrowing or Return	To calculate the cost of rental
Customer Reference	To link with the customer file and show which customer has hired it.

(c) For four different fields described in (b), describe an appropriate validation technique.   [4]

(c) Customer Reference will be validated with either a range check or a
     check digit.
     Customer Name will be checked with a character check as all characters
     should be alphabetic.
     Address is difficult to check but the postcode could be checked with a
     format check.
     Date could use a format check and a range check.
     Number of videos on hire should be numerical and there will be a range
     check.
     Video Code will be validated check digit.
     Video title will also be difficult, but there could be a length check.

Try to pick fields that have a clear method of validation. You will get full marks for any four of these.

Practice examination questions

1 A large mail order company operates from a centrally placed site, which includes office accommodation, and a large warehouse. Glossy catalogues, which each contain over a thousand pages of descriptions of goods, are delivered to their customers twice yearly. Customers may order by mail, telephone, fax or e-mail. Payment can be made by cheque, by regular standing order, or, where appropriate, by tele-banking. The company employs a total of about two thousand staff. This includes office, warehouse, marketing and buying personnel. The company makes use of computing facilities as much as possible.

The company holds information about its employees on computer, in two main databases; one holds payroll information, and the other holds personnel information.

(a) Describe four essential fields which you would expect to be present in the payroll table (file). [4]

(b) Describe four essential fields which you would expect to be present in the personnel table (file). [4]

(c) Give an example of one action which would cause the payroll file to be updated, and one action which would cause the personnel file to be updated. Describe briefly the method of updating which would be appropriate for each database. [6]

(d) Give three precautions which the company must take in keeping data of this nature. [3]

OCR 1999, 6811

2 A mail order company has agents who work from home. When an agent wishes to order some goods they fill in an order form and send it to the company by post. When an order is received at the company, the data is keyed into the computer system. The order is validated and stored in the Order File. The Order File is then processed against the Stock File to produce despatch notes which are sent to the warehouse and a report of items that are unavailable is produced. The following is a diagram showing the processes, files and printouts involved.

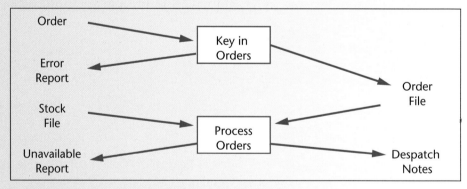

An order has the following fields which are keyed in:

Order Number
Agent Number
Date of Order
Quantity
Unit Price

(a) How should each of the above fields be validated by the Key in Orders process? [6]

(b) Give two reasons for an item appearing on the Unavailable Report. [2]

NEAB 1998, CPO2

3 A fundholding general practice consists of five doctors, a nurse, a practice manager and several part-time receptionists.

A **local area network** has been installed for maintaining patient records and for financial management.

The patient data are held on a database which can be accessed from reception, from the doctors consulting rooms and by the nurse.

The practice manager uses an integrated financial package via his own terminal.

(a) What is a local area network? [2]

(b) The database is managed by a *database management system* (DBMS). What is a database management system? [2]

(c) State **three** advantages of using a database for patient records rather than each type of user having their own separate application program and files, such as an appointment booking program for the receptionists and a full medical record system for the doctors. [3]

(d) Medical details are confidential between doctor and patient, so different levels of access to the database are required for the different types of user. Explain how a user would identify himself or herself to the DBMS. [2]

(e) How should the data stored on the network be protected against loss by fire? [2]

(f) Explain carefully why each patient is given a reference number when they register with the practice. [3]

(g) The financial package includes an advanced spreadsheet facility. How could this software be used by the practice manager for planning and budgeting? [2]

AEB 1997, Paper 1

4 A common activity in computerised systems is to bring up to date details held in the records of a disk master file, using new data collected in a transaction file. The transaction file is held on magnetic tape and contains details of a day's transactions, which have previously been checked (verified and validated). This file is sorted onto a disk file which is then used to produce a new master file from the old one. Any errors are listed in a report.

Represent this activity diagrammatically, showing the flow of data and the processes involved. [5]

NEAB 1999, CP01

Chapter 7

Systems development

The following topics are covered in this chapter:

- *The systems life cycle*
- *Analysis*
- *Design*

7.1 The systems life cycle

After studying this section you should be able to:

- *describe the stages of development of a computerised system*

LEARNING SUMMARY

The life cycle

AQA	M3
EDEXCEL	M2, M3
OCR	M3
WJEC	CP1, CP3

The development of a system goes through a number of phases:

- Problem definition – a problem will be identified by a user.
- Feasibility study – the problem is investigated to decide whether a new system is required.
- Analysis – the requirements will be analysed and a requirements specification produced. This document forms the contract between the customer and the developer of the system.
- Design – the design can now be produced (see below for techniques used).
- Construction – the system is constructed by writing the necessary programs and testing them using appropriate software tools.
- Testing – the system will be fully tested.
- Implementation – the system will be implemented and training will be provided to the satisfaction of the user.
- Maintenance – it will be necessary to maintain most systems to meet changing requirements and to solve problems that arise during operation.
- Evaluation – the system must be evaluated from time to time to ensure that it continues to meet the requirements of the user. The evaluation may well come up with another problem that could start the process again.

These phases follow one another in sequence, so the development can be shown by Figure 29.

> You will come across variations on this systems life cycle. Do not worry about this. The main point is to understand the principle of the systems life cycle.

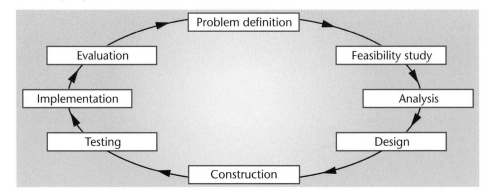

Figure 29

> **KEY POINT**
>
> The development of a system is cyclical, that is once one cycle is completed another cycle may well start.

Progress check

When a systems life cycle is completed it is common practice to restart the cycle. Why is the systems life cycle a circular process?

The systems life cycle is a circular process as the evaluation of a project inevitably leads to suggestions for improvements to be made. These improvements can only be put in place by starting the systems life cycle once again.

7.2 Analysis

After studying this section you should be able to:

- *describe methods of obtaining user requirements*
- *draw a system flowchart*
- *evaluate the feasibility of a computer-based solution*
- *derive a data model*
- *suggest implementation strategies*
- *identify possible maintenance requirements*

> **LEARNING SUMMARY**

Gathering information

AQA	M3
EDEXCEL	M2, M3
OCR	M3
WJEC	CP1, CP3

The methods that can be used to gather data include:

- Inspecting existing records
- Observing current practice
- Interviewing
- Questionnaires.

Having gathered the data it is now possible to consider the processing that will be required.

Documentation

AQA	M3
EDEXCEL	M2, M3
OCR	M3
WJEC	CP1, CP3

There are various methods of documenting the flow of data around a system. One method is to use a system flowchart. This method uses a rectangle to denote some process that takes place (normally a computer program) and descriptive symbols to describe the storage or input/output of data. For example:

Process

Disk

Tape

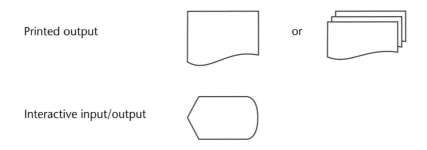

Printed output   or

Interactive input/output

You may also see generic symbols that are used when the device is unspecified such as:

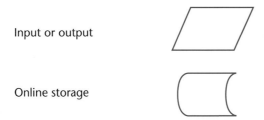

Input or output

Online storage

A flowchart to show orders being entered online and stored on a magnetic disk might be:

> Do not be too bothered about using the correct symbols. As long as they are reasonably appropriate you will be OK. The important points to get right are the data flows.

Orders → Accept orders → Order File

There would normally be some checking of the orders, in which case there would be errors fed back to the data entry device. If this is the case the flowchart might become:

Orders ⟷ Validate orders → Order File

The arrows represent the flow of data.

KEY POINT

Estimating viability

AQA	M3
EDEXCEL	M2, M3
OCR	M3
WJEC	CP1, CP3

> You are unlikely to be asked about specific values for costs and benefits but you should be aware of the likely areas where they may be.

It will also be necessary to estimate the costs and benefits to establish the viability of the project. Costs are likely to include:

- Hardware
- Software
- Training
- Implementation
- Maintenance.

Benefits might include:

- Reduced staffing
- Better service to customers
- Management information
- Faster processing that could speed up payments from customers.

Data model

AQA	M3
EDEXCEL	M2, M3
OCR	M2, M3
WJEC	CP1, CP3

> There are other symbols used to denote a many relationship, such as an arrowhead, but the crow's foot would appear to be the most popular.

A data model will represent the relationship between different parts of a database. It consists of **entities** (data items) and **relationships**. The entities are shown as rectangles and the relationships are drawn as lines that connect entities. Relationships can be one-to-one, one-to-many or many-to-many, and a 'crow's foot' can be used to show a many relationship. An example might be:

where this denotes three entities, student, course and tutor. It shows that a student can enrol on many courses and that a course can have many students. It shows that a tutor can teach on many courses but that a course has only one tutor.

> You must look carefully at the application described in the question as the key will be to get the relationships correct.
>
> **KEY POINT**

Testing

AQA	M3
EDEXCEL	M2, M3
OCR	M2, M3
WJEC	CP1, CP3

> The importance of rigorous testing is often badly understood. It should not be confused with debugging. Testing only starts when the system appears to operate correctly, that is when debugging has finished.

Testing is regarded by the computer industry as vitally important, so much so that the industry employs large numbers of people to do nothing else. There are various testing strategies you should be aware of:

- Dry run – manually work through a program or system step by step.
- Unit test – test each part of the system individually.
- Integration test – put it all together and test the complete system.

The test data should be chosen carefully. They should test the system for normal running as well as testing for erroneous data. The most important area is to find the limits (or boundaries) of the data. Tests should then be performed at the boundary, just inside the boundary and just outside the boundary. An example might be a credit limit on a bank account. There should be a test to take the account to just below the credit limit, a test to take it to the credit limit and a test to take it just over the credit limit.

Once the system is tested to the satisfaction of the team that develops it, the system will be passed to the user of the system who will conduct their own series of tests before they accept it. This is known as **acceptance testing**.

> Testing consists of various stages. We initially test the individual programs. The tested programs can then be combined to test subsystems. The tested subsystems can then be combined finally to test the complete system.
>
> **KEY POINT**

Implementation

AQA	M3
EDEXCEL	M2, M3
OCR	M2, M3
WJEC	CP1, CP3

The new system can be implemented either as a whole or in parts. The problem is that an organisation cannot change instantly to a new method of working as existing records will have to be entered into the computer and this may take some time. There are two important approaches:

- Implement the system department by department.
- Dual run the new system alongside the old system.

Dual running has the advantage that the customer can be confident that the new system is operating successfully before removing the old system. It is, however, expensive to run both systems at the same time.

Maintenance

AQA	M3
EDEXCEL	M2, M3
OCR	M2, M3
WJEC	CP1, CP3

An enormous amount of effort is put into maintaining existing systems. There are three types of maintenance:

- Perfective maintenance – making the system easier to use or adding new facilities.
- Adaptive maintenance – making changes to the system following changes in the working environment. This may be because of changes in working practices or changes in legislation.
- Corrective maintenance – changes owing to errors discovered in the original system.

In order that maintenance can take place efficiently it is vital that systems are correctly documented. There will normally be:

- Systems specification with all system flowcharts, entity relationship diagrams, inputs, outputs, processes and a log of tests carried out.
- Program documentation with program specification, program listing, structure charts or pseudocode, and a log of tests carried out.
- Operations manual to describe the initial setup procedures, the normal running procedures, security procedures and recovery procedures in the event of system failure.
- User manual giving instructions on the operation of the system including screen shots, report layouts, description of options available and explanation of error messages.

> As more and more systems are brought into use the amount of effort put into maintenance increases. As a result there is far more effort put into maintenance than into new systems.

All the above will need to be constantly updated as maintenance proceeds. **Configuration management tools** are available to assist with this task.

> Systems need continual maintenance owing to the changing circumstances that businesses find themselves in.

KEY POINT

Progress check

> As we are asked for the five main stages we must decide which are the key stages. Note that a description is requested, so naming them will not get you the marks.

Describe the five main stages in the full life cycle of a computerised system.

Requirements analysis – the costs and benefits of the new system will be established and a requirements specification will be produced. This report will cover the existing system, the cost/benefit analysis of the new system and suggestions as to how to proceed.
Systems analysis – if the requirements specification is accepted then the existing system is analysed in detail using interviews, questionnaires and/or observation. Data flows are analysed and documented.
Systems design – the reports, files, inputs and processing stages are designed in detail and documented. A testing strategy is decided upon.
Construction – the programs are written, debugged and documented.
Testing – each part of the system will be tested individually followed by full system tests. Finally the system will be acceptance tested by the customer.

7.3 Design

After studying this section you should be able to:

- *document a design*
- *define prototyping*
- *specify a design that meets the requirements of the problem*

Basic principles

AQA	M3
EDEXCEL	M2, M3
OCR	M2, M3
WJEC	CP1, CP3

When designing the system you have to take into account the hardware and software that are available. You must also design the human – computer interface in such a way that the user will find it straightforward to use.

Documentation

AQA	M3
EDEXCEL	M1
OCR	M3
WJEC	CP2

Documentation should be appropriate to the design feature that is being described.

- System flowcharts – as described previously, these describe the flow of data around the system.
- Entity relationship diagrams – as described previously, these show the design of a data model.
- Structure diagrams – these are a means of showing the design of a program or system. They consist of charts showing the system or program broken down into a number of levels (Figure 30).

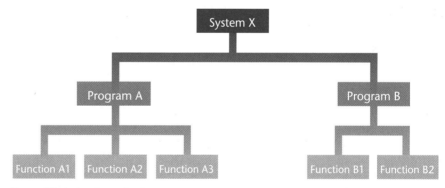

Figure 30 A structure chart

- Hierarchy charts – these can be used to show a menu hierarchy or a directory hierarchy (Figure 31).

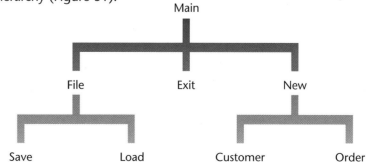

Figure 31 A sample menu hierarchy

It is important that you can document a system appropriately, but if you are not sure of the correct box or symbol this is less important than showing the correct processes and relationships.

- Pseudocode – this is used to describe algorithms (Figure 32).

```
While not end of report file
    Begin
            Read next record on report file
            Print contents of record
    EndWhile
```

Figure 32 An example of pseudocode

Prototyping

AQA	M3
EDEXCEL	M2, M3
OCR	M3
WJEC	CP1, CP3

A prototype is only worth producing either if it can be done with very little effort or if the analyst is able to reuse much of the work in the final product.

Often a customer is unclear of their exact requirements. In this case a prototype may be produced that will be a model of the system but having limited facilities. A prototype may take the form of:

- A set of screens that show the user what might be possible
- A system with limited functionality
- An existing system that might be modified.

A prototype can be very beneficial to the customer as they can get a clearer idea of the proposed system.

Human–computer interface (HCI)

AQA	M3
EDEXCEL	M2, M3
OCR	M3
WJEC	CP1, CP3

The HCI must be designed carefully. There are a number of options available:

- Keyboard input that may involve a command language
- WIMP environment
- Speech
- Direct manipulation, embed the system within a device.

Sometimes a command line interface (using a keyboard) is appropriate. More often a WIMP (windows icon mouse pointer) interface is appropriate. In the case of a WIMP environment it is important that standards are adhered to so that the user can be confident of consistency between different screens. Examples of such standards are that FILE should be the first dropdown menu item, radio buttons should be used as a selection device, and so on.

Always take into account the person who will use the system.

Progress check

A common mistake is to draw a program flowchart when a system flowchart is requested. Read these questions carefully and make sure you give the examiner the correct type of chart.

Student attendance is recorded daily on OMR forms. The forms are batched and the data transferred onto a disk file Weekly_Attendance. Once a week an update program is executed to transfer the attendance data to the indexed sequential file Student_Register and to produce a printed list of absences.

1 What is the technique known as OMR?
2 Draw a system flowchart for the weekly update.

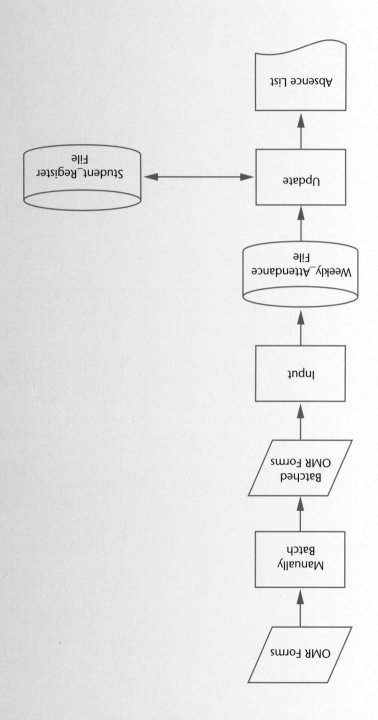

2

1 Optical mark recognition (OMR) is a technique used to enter data into a computer system. Marks are made on a prepared form using a pen or pencil and they are detected by an optical mark reader.

99

Sample questions and model answers

1

An industrial cleaning company employs some of its workers at an hourly rate and uses a computer to produce their payslips and pay cheques each week. The payroll program updates the sequential Payroll Master File from a validated Transaction File which has previously been sorted into the correct order. The payroll program retrieves personal details such as name, address and rate of pay from the Employee Master File which is organised indexed sequentially. All the computer files are held on disk. The diagram illustrates the data flow of this system.

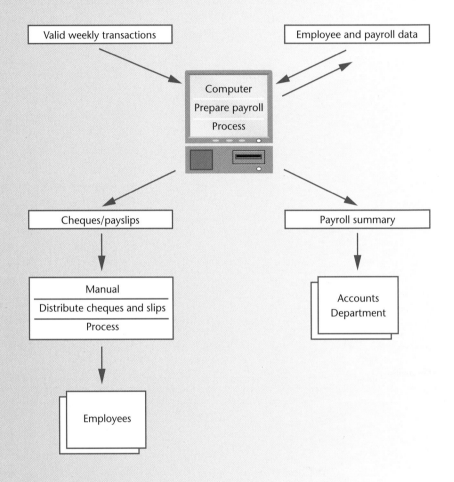

Note that a systems flowchart is required. Do not make the common mistake of drawing a program flowchart.

(a) Draw a systems flowchart for the weekly payroll.   [8]

(a)

An indexed sequential file can be accessed directly (via the index) or sequentially (as the records are stored in sequence). This question is about using the indexed sequential file in two different ways.

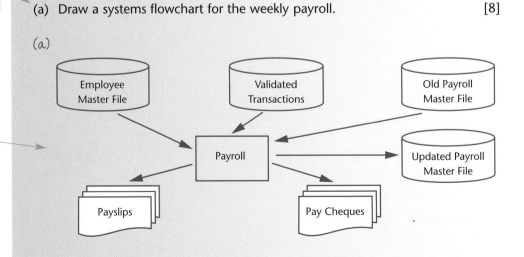

(b) One reason why the payroll update is performed sequentially is the high hit rate for this process. What is *hit rate*, and how is it calculated? [3]

(b) The hit rate measures the proportion of the records on the Master File that are being accessed and is calculated as follows:

$$\frac{\text{No. of records accessed}}{\text{No. of records on the file}} \times 100\%$$

(c) Another advantage of sequential processing is that a separate run to backup the Master File is unnecessary. Explain why. [3]

(c) A grandfather, father, son system will be used for the Master File. As the two previous Master Files are kept together with the old Transaction Files a backup is automatically in place.

(d) Why is it beneficial for the Employee Master file to be indexed as well as sequentially organised? [2]

AEB 1996, Paper 1

(d) There will be other applications that use the Employee Master File, for example Personnel. They are likely to need online access to this file and this will require direct access. Only an indexed sequential file offers both direct access and sequential access.

This part requires you to consider other applications. Be aware that one application may be affected by the needs of others.

2

User interfaces have gradually become more and more oriented to the needs of users over recent years.

(a) Briefly describe **three** features of user interfaces which have been developed and explain how each has benefited the user. [3]

(a) Appropriate icons together with a mouse and pointer make it easy to select actions.

An online help facility, often available from a hot key such as F1, makes life easier when a user requires information about the system.

Hierarchical menus enable the user to find programs or other features quickly.

This question asks you to apply your knowledge of a current operating system's user interface (probably Windows) and to suggest improvements. Any sensible suggestions are likely to get you some marks.

(b) Describe **two** ways in which user interfaces need to be developed further to make computers accessible and friendly to untrained users. [2]

(b) Voice input and speech synthesis will make it easier for users to communicate with the computer.

Improved help messages and/or explanations when things go wrong will make it easier to use a computer system.

Practice examination questions

1 In a data entry process, data is manually entered at the keyboard from documents validated and then saved to disk if no errors are found. A printed report is generated if errors do occur during this validation process.
   Draw a *system flow chart* to show these processes. [5]

   AEB 1999, Paper 2

2 During its lifetime, computer software will often require *maintenance*.
   (a) What is meant by the term *maintenance*? [1]
   (b) Maintenance of software is often classified as *perfective, adaptive* or *corrective*. Briefly explain the meaning of these terms and, for **each** one, give an example of a situation which might require that type of maintenance. [6]
   (c) State **three** items you would expect to find in the documentation that would help maintenance. [3]

   NEAB 1999, CP01

3 Many computer systems involve a *batch update*. This operates as follows:

   Details of transactions are entered using a keyboard, and validated immediately; any error is displayed on the screen, corrected and re-entered. Valid data is stored on tape to form a transaction file.

   Each evening, the transaction file is sorted and stored on disk. The sorted file is then used to update a master file stored on disk. During update, other errors may be reported on a printer.

   Represent this batch update process in diagrammatic form, showing the inputs and outputs, the flow of data, and the necessary processes. [8]

   NEAB 1998, CP01

Chapter 8

Programming

- *Generations of program language*
- *Data types*
- *Programming statements*
- *Algorithms*

8.1 Generations of program language

After studying this section you should be able to:

- *discuss the development of programming languages*
- *describe machine code language and assembly language*
- *explain the term 'high-level language'*

LEARNING SUMMARY

Development of programming languages

AQA	M1
EDEXCEL	M2
OCR	M1
WJEC	CP1

Machine code

All computers execute **machine code** programs. A machine code instruction consists of a binary code that represents an operation optionally followed by one or more addresses. An instruction to move data from 0000110000001111 to 0000110000001100 might be

| 01101001 | 0000110000001111 | 0000110000001100 |
| MOVE OPERATION | ADDRESS 1 | ADDRESS 2 |

Assembly language

In the early days of commercial computing all programs were written in assembly code.

It is very difficult for humans to work in machine code so **assembly language** has been developed. An assembly language instruction has a mnemonic (a shorthand description) to describe the operation and allows the programmer to name memory locations. The machine code instruction above might be written as

    MOV   INAMOUNT, OUTAMOUNT

The assembly language instruction is converted into the machine code instruction by an **assembler program**. Machine code is often referred to as a 1st generation language and assembly language as 2nd generation.

High-level languages

Assembly code is not ideal for most software as the language requires a large number of instructions to perform relatively simple tasks. As a result a series of high-level languages have been designed (often known as 3rd generation). A high-level language is designed around the problem to be solved rather than the machine code. A compiler or interpreter converts a high-level language into machine code and one high-level language instruction will generate many machine code instructions. There are many different high-level languages but some of the common types are:

> You do not need to be familiar with all these programming languages, but you should be aware that they exist.

- Business languages – COBOL has been the main language for business programming, having good file processing and report-writing capabilities.
- Scientific languages – FORTRAN and ALGOL were developed for scientific work.
- Educational languages – PASCAL and LOGO have been developed as languages to use when teaching the principles of programming.
- Systems programming – C has been developed to write operating systems and associated systems programs.
- Object oriented programming – C++, DELPHI, SMALLTALK and EIFFEL are modern object oriented programming languages.
- Artificial intelligence – PROLOG has been developed to implement these applications.

A language is specified by:

- **Syntax** – a set of rules for combining elements of a language into a form the compiler can understand.
- **Semantics** – a term for the meaning of the statements used in program.

The syntax of a programming language can be written in the form of a **grammar**

> You need to have studied a high-level language to understand the process of program development.

KEY POINT

Progress check

1 Explain what is meant by a programming language.
2 Distinguish between low-level and high-level programming languages.
3 What must happen to the source code of a program before it can be executed, and why is this necessary?

1 A programming language is a set of rules (syntax and semantics) for writing sets of instructions on a computer. (Full marks would probably be obtained without mentioning syntax and semantics.)

2 A low-level language is oriented towards a particular processor, a high-level language is oriented towards a particular problem type. (An alternative answer is low-level requires knowledge of machine architecture whereas high-level is machine independent. Or, low-level has a one-to-one correspondence with machine code instructions, high-level has a one-to-many correspondence. Or, low-level is machine-oriented, high-level is human-oriented.)

3 The program needs to be translated into a machine code as computers can only execute machine code. (Note that you must make both points to get full marks. One mark was for stating that translation is necessary and one mark for the reason why.)

8.2 Data types

After studying this section you should be able to:

- *explain the advantages of named constants and variables*
- *describe primitive data types*
- *describe simple data structures*
- *describe user-defined data types*
- *recognise and use abstract data types*

LEARNING SUMMARY

The different data types

AQA	M1
EDEXCEL	M2
OCR	M1
WJEC	CP1

Simple data types

In a high-level language a **constant** or a **variable** represents one or more memory locations where data can be stored. The contents of a constant are fixed but the contents of a variable can be altered. A variable or constant will be of a specified type (integer, character, and so on) depending on the data to be stored. Most languages offer some primitive data types such as:

- Integer – to store whole numbers.
- Real – to store values that contain digits after the decimal point.
- Character – to store a single character.
- Boolean – to store one of the two values, True or False.

Complex data types

There are other types in different languages but the above are the main group of simple types. A language other than Pascal may have slightly different names. You should use the names you are familiar with.

It is possible to use more complex types:

- Array – a collection of items, each of which can be accessed directly using a subscript, for example Table[5] refers to the fifth item in the array Table.
- String – naturally an array of characters but sometimes offered as a special type.
- Record – a collection of variables that hold related data.

Complex types can be specified by the programmer and named. In this case the type is known as a **user-defined type**.

Abstract data types

It is not necessary to understand the workings of ADTs for AS level.

Abstract data types (ADTs) are complex data types that have operations associated with them. To access an ADT ask it to perform some operation, e.g. a stack that has the operations Push and Pop. To add an item to the stack you use Push and to remove an item from the stack you would use Pop. Abstract data types include:

- Queue – a first in first out (FIFO) data structure. Items are retrieved in the same sequence that they were added.
- Stack – a last in first out (LIFO) data structure. Items are retrieved in the reverse sequence.
- Binary search tree – items are added in any sequence. Items can be viewed in ascending key sequence. A useful structure that automatically sorts the data.

Progress check

1 What is meant by the Boolean data type?
2 Give two other examples of data types.

2 Integer and character.

1 Variable with only two possible values, e.g. true/false.

8.3 Programming statements

After studying this section you should be able to:

- *state the various types of statement available in a high-level language*
- *describe the operation of the statements of a high-level language*
- *describe the use of parameters*

LEARNING SUMMARY

Most high-level languages are procedural and will typically have the following statements. We shall use Pascal as our sample language here but other languages have similar statements. Examiners may use Pascal but they are just as likely to use some pseudolanguage that looks like Pascal. Do not worry if the program statements in AS questions are not exactly the ones you are used to.

Constant definitions

AQA	M1
EDEXCEL	M2
OCR	M1
WJEC	CP1

It is often convenient to be able to name some constant values, for example you might want to name the maximum number of items to be allowed in a program. This could be achieved in Pascal by defining MaxItems as a constant, for example:

    MaxItems = 500;

This makes a program easier to read and makes it simple to change the maximum number of items at a later stage.

Variable definitions

AQA	M1
EDEXCEL	M2
OCR	M1
WJEC	CP1

Variable definitions allow memory locations to be named. In a high-level language a variable will also be associated with a data type that will specify the type of data that can be stored. Examples are:

    Count: integer;
    Amount: real;
    Accept: boolean;
    MenuChoice: character;

Type definitions

AQA	M1
EDEXCEL	M2
OCR	M1
WJEC	CP1

As well as a number of standard data types it is possible to define additional data types. An example might be:

    MyColours = [Red, Green, Blue, Yellow];

Assignment statement

AQA	M1
EDEXCEL	M2
OCR	M1
WJEC	CP1

A value is computed and then assigned to a variable in the memory of the computer. An example might be:

    x := y + 2;

Selection statement

AQA	M1
EDEXCEL	M2
OCR	M1
WJEC	CP1

When the program has to make a decision as to the next operation to be carried out a selection statement is used. The simplest selection statement is the if statement. An example is:

```
if (amount > creditlimit)
    then writeln('Amount greater than creditlimit – authorisation required')
    else writeln('Authorisation not required');
```

This statement will cause the program to output 'Amount greater than creditlimit – authorisation required' if the value of the variable amount is greater than the value of the variable creditlimit. If the value of amount is not greater than creditlimit then the output will be 'Authorisation not required'.

A more complex selection statement is the case statement (sometimes called a switch statement). This statement causes the computer to select one of a list of options, for example:

```
Case MenuChoice of
    'A' : writeln('You have chosen Add');
    'C' : writeln('You have chosen Change');
    'D' : writeln('You have chosen Delete');
end; {case}
```

Iteration

AQA	M1
EDEXCEL	M2
OCR	M1
WJEC	CP1

An iteration statement allows the execution of a series of statements a number of times (often called a loop). There are two main types of loop:

- While/Repeat – used when the number of loops to be taken is unknown on entry
- For – used when the number of loops is known in advance.

Both the while and repeat statements loop until some condition is met. The difference is that the repeat statement is used when the series of statement must be executed at least once. The while statement may not execute the statements at all if the condition is not met. An example is:

```
total = 0;
writeln ('Please enter next value to be totalled. Enter –1 if finished');
readln(amount)
while (amount <> –1) do
    begin
        total := total + amount;
        writeln ('Please enter next value to be totalled. Enter –1 if finished');
        readln(amount)
        end; {while}
    writeln ('The total is ',total);
```

The above statements will accept a number of values, add them up and output the total. This will operate successfully when the user enters –1 as the first value. If we are certain that there will always be at least one value we might use a repeat loop as follows:

```
total = 0;
writeln ('Please enter the first value to be totalled.');
readln(amount)
repeat
        total := total + amount;
        writeln ('Please enter next value to be totalled. Enter –1 if finished');
        readln(amount)
until (amount = –1);
writeln ('The total is ',total);
```

Procedure and function

AQA   M1
EDEXCEL   M2
OCR   M1
WJEC   CP1

Procedure and function allow the specification of a series of statements that are to be executed together. This allows the development of 'subprograms' that perform specific tasks. The only difference between a procedure and a function is that a function returns a value and a procedure does not. An example of a function might be:

```
Function Square(x : integer) : integer;
Begin
   Square := x * x
End; {square}
```

This function will accept a parameter (declared as x in the example) and return the value squared. It might be used as follows:

```
Y := Square(5);
```

This would execute the function Square (we say that we **call** the function) with x set to 5. Square will return the value 25 and so Y will be set to 25. An important feature of procedures is the ability to use **local variables**. Any variable declared inside a procedure or function (and this includes parameters) are said to be local to that procedure or function. This means that they are not recognised outside the procedure or function. The part of the program in which a variable is recognised is called the **scope** of the variable. An example of a procedure might be:

```
Procedure PrintSquare(x: integer);
Begin
   Writeln(x*x)
End; {PrintSquare}
```

Note that this procedure will output the squared value so it does not have anything to return. This might be used as follows:

```
PrintSquare(4);
```

This would cause the program to output the value 16.

You will only become familiar with the use of these statements by writing computer programs. It is often said that 'programming is not a spectator sport'. You have to do it yourself to become skilful.

> You need to be aware of the use of the above types of statements in your chosen language.

KEY POINT

Progress check

Opposite is a fragment of a
computer program:

1 For the fragment shown, identify
the following:
   (a) the local variable
   (b) the global variable
   (c) the parameter.

2 Describe briefly what is meant by
   (a) local variables
   (b) global variables
   (c) parameters .

3 What is the benefit of using
parameters in procedures?

```
Integer n_records
        .
        .
procedure display_record(n)
integer linenum
        .
        .
if (n > n_records) then
        display_error_message_box()
endif
        .
        .
endproc
```

3 They enable procedures to be of general use.

(c) Values that are passed into or out of a procedure. The values are placed in formal parameters
   (sometimes known as placeholders).
(b) The scope of a global variable is the whole program
2 (a) The scope of a local variable is the procedure in which it is declared

(c) n is the parameter.
(b) n_records is the global variable
1 (a) linnenum is the local variable

8.4 Algorithms

After studying this section you should be able to:

- *hand trace simple algorithms*
- *describe a binary search*

Definition and execution

AQA	M1
EDEXCEL	M2
OCR	M1
WJEC	CP1

An algorithm is a series of operations that perform some result. It is often written in pseudocode. Pseudocode is a method of writing what are, in effect, program statements without adhering to the strict rules of any particular programming language. You should be prepared to determine the results of executing a given algorithm manually (a dry run). When executing a given algorithm you may be asked to produce a trace table. This is a simple table that has a column for every variable that is used. Every time a variable changes its value it is updated by adding a new row to the table.

Binary search

| WJEC | CP1 |

A binary search is an algorithm that is used to find an item in an ordered array. It is much faster than a linear search (checking each entry in turn from the first to the last). In a binary search the middle item is selected (in the case of an array with 33 entries, the middle item will be the 16th entry). If the item is the sought item the search is complete. If the sought item is larger than the middle item all the items smaller than the middle can be ignored and the search continues using the items larger than the middle item. If the sought item is smaller than the middle item the items larger than the middle item can be ignored and the search continues using the items smaller than the middle item. In this way the number of items to be searched is halved each time until the item is found or the search fails when there are no more items to be checked. A pseudocode procedure for a binary search on an array is:

The array is called Arr.
The number of items is N.
Found and failed are boolean variables.
Top, bottom and middle are integer values.
ItemWanted is the item that is sought.

Procedure search
```
    found:   = False
    failed:  = False
    top:     = N
    bottom: = 1
    repeat
            Middle: = integer part of ((top + bottom)/2)
            if Arr[middle] = ItemWanted
                then Found: = true
                else
                        if bottom > top
                                then failed: = true
                                Else
```

```
                                        if Arr[middle] < itemWanted
                                            then bottom: = middle + 1
                                            else top: = middle –1
                                        endif
                            endif
                    endif
            until found = true or failed = true
        endproc
```

Progress check

A 7-element array, NAMES[1 .. 7], initially contains

PHIL, NICK, WAI, LIZ, HAMID, JO and AYSHA.

The algorithm below is used to process the array.
(The function **INT**(X) returns the integer part of the variable X, i.e. with all digits after the decimal point removed; the procedure **EXC**(X1, X2) exchanges the values held in the variables X1 and X2.)

```
MAX := 7
D := MAX
repeat
        D := INT( ( D / 2 ) + 0.5 )
        for PTR := 1 to ( MAX - D )
                if NAMES[ PTR ] > NAMES[ PTR + D ] then
                        EXC( NAMES[ PTR ], NAMES[ PTR + D ] )
                endif
        endfor
until D = 1
```

Show the effect of executing this algorithm by copying and completing the trace table below. Show the value of each variable whenever a value is assigned to it.

NAMES										
1	*2*	*3*	*4*	*5*	*6*	*7*	*MAX*	*D*	*PTR*	*Comment*
PHIL	NICK	WAI	LIZ	HAMID	JO	AYSHA				

Answers overleaf

Answers

NAMES							MAX	D	PTR	Comment
1	**2**	**3**	**4**	**5**	**6**	**7**				
PHIL	NICK	WAI	LIZ	HAMID	JO	AYSHA	7	7		
								4		
									1	
HAMID				PHIL					2	
	JO				NICK				3	
		AYSHA				WAI				endfor
										repeat, d<>1
								2		
									1	
AYSHA		HAMID							2	no swap
									3	no swap
									4	no swap
									5	no swap
										endfor
										repeat, d<>1
								1		
									1	no swap
									2	
	HAMID	JO							3	no swap
									4	no swap
									5	
				NICK	PHIL				6	no swap
										endfor
										d=1, terminates

Final order is AYSHA, HAMID, JO, LIZ, NICK, PHIL, WAI.

Sample questions and model answers

1

The following section of pseudocode illustrates the process of converting a positive integer value into a character string for output.

DIGITS is a one-dimensional array; I, K, X and Y are integer variables. Each element of DIGITS can be used to store an integer equivalent to the code of a single ASCII character. The value to be processed is initially stored in X.

```
Initialise    I=0
Repeat        Add 1 to I
              Assign the whole number part of X/10 to Y
              calculate X–10*Y and Assign result to K
              calculate K+48 (the ASCII code for the digit held in K)
              And Assign to element I of DIGITS
              Assign X = Y
Until X = 0
```

(a) Copy and complete the following dry-run table for this algorithm given that the initial value of X is 7046.

				Elements of DIGITS					
X	*I*	*Y*	*K*	*1*	*2*	*3*	*4*	*5*	*6*

[9]

> It is easy to guess the results of an algorithm incorrectly. You need to work through the algorithm very carefully, noting down each change to the variables as you go. There is no substitute for working through several algorithms to improve your skill in this area.

(a)

				Elements of DIGITS					
X	*I*	*Y*	*K*	*1*	*2*	*3*	*4*	*5*	*6*
7046	0								
704	1	704	6	54					
70	2	70	4		52				
7	3	7	0			48			
0	4	0	7				55		

(b) Write down what would be printed if the following algorithm is now used to output the contents of DIGITS, given that I now equals 4.

```
Initialise K = 1
While         K less than 1
              Print element K of DIGITS
              Newline
              Add 1 to K
Endwhile
```

[4]

> Again, you need to be careful. It is easy to miss the fact that only three numbers are output.

(b) 6
4
0

(c) Rewrite the pseudocode given in part (b) so that the original integer given in X is printed correctly.

[3]

AEB 1997, Paper 1

> The main points to recognise are that the digits are in reverse order. It is often necessary to reverse the order of items and this is one way to do it.

```
c  Initialise K = 0
   While K < I
        Print DIGITS (I–k)
        Add 1 to K
   Endwhile
   Newline
```

Practice examination questions

1 (a) What is meant by a *high-level programming language*? [2]

(b) There is a large number of high-level languages: FORTRAN, COBOL, BASIC, etc. Why are there so many? [2]

NEAB 1998, CP01

2 A computer program contains the following fragment:

Boolean: LY

Integer: Y

...

LY := ((Y **mod** 4 = 0) **AND** (**NOT** (Y **mod** 100 = 0) **OR** (Y **mod** 400 = 0))

(The function A **mod** B returns the remainder when A is divided by B, e.g. 11 **mod** 3 returns the value 2.)

(a) What is meant by a Boolean variable? [1]

(b) What value would be assigned to the variable LY, if the variable Y contains

(i) 1999 [1]

(ii) 2000 [1]

NEAB 1999, CP01

3 The following section of pseudocode processes a one-dimensional integer array called List. The numbers in List are stored in ascending order, and x, Low, High, Middle are all integer variables. (The function Int returns the whole number part of its parameter.)

```
Proc Process(Low, High, x)
    Found ← False
        Repeat
                Middle ← Int((Low + High)/2)
                If List(Middle) = x
                Then Found ← True
                Else If List(Middle) > x
                Then High ← Middle – 1
                Else Low ← Middle + 1    {List(Middle) < x}
        Until Found = True
```

(a) Complete the following dry-run table for Process (1, 10, 19), given that the integers in the list are: 2, 4, 6, 7, 11, 13, 19, 21, 27, 29.

Low	High	Middle	Found
1	10		

[7]

(b) What type of routine does this pseudocode define? [1]

AEB 1999 Paper 2

Practice examination answers

1 Applications of computers

1 The rapid increase in databases and networked computers has caused people to be concerned about the data stored about them. They are concerned that the data could be misused without them knowing about it. They were also concerned that the data held could be misleading or inaccurate and these data could be passed on to another organisation (such as a financial institution) without their consent. The Data Protection Act 1984 gives the individual some rights:

2 Right to be informed that personal data are held.
Right to be supplied with a copy of any such personal data.
Compensation for inaccuracy in the stored data.
Compensation for loss of data.
Compensation for unauthorised disclosure of the data.
Rectification or erasure if data are inaccurate.
Right to have data deleted if out of date.
[Any three of the above would get you the marks.]

3 The principles that appear to have been broken are:

The data must be accurate and up-to-date.
The data must be used only for the purpose they were given.
The data must be held no longer than is necessary.
The data must be obtained fairly and lawfully.
[Any two of these would get you the marks.]

4 (a) Workers can have flexible working hours.
Workers do not waste time travelling to work.
Workers can save money by not travelling to work.
Workers can live in a pleasant part of the country.

(b) There will be less congestion and pollution with fewer journeys.
It could revitalise country areas.

5 (a) Provide multi-column layouts as used in a typical newspaper.
Ability to import pictures and diagrams to illustrate articles.
A spell checker and grammar checker to produce a professional result.
(Almost any reasonable set of three features would get you the marks.)
(b) (i) Buy a standard software package
(ii) Bespoke software provides exactly what is required.
Buying a package will be cheaper.

2 Computer hardware

1   The inkjet printer is cheaper to purchase than a laser printer.
     The inkjet is more expensive to operate owing to the high cost of ink cartridges.

2   (a)   A buffer is a temporary store for data being transferred between two devices, typically between memory and a peripheral, because of a difference in the speed of the two devices.
     (b)   An example might be part of memory used as a buffer when data are transferred to a magnetic disk.

3   A faster processing speed is desirable as it will increase the number of operations that can be performed in one second. Some software requires a high processor speed in order to perform satisfactorily (particularly multimedia and graphics).

     A computer system must have enough memory to store the software and the data that is to be processed. Large programs need a large amount of memory.

     The backing store will be used to store all the software, including the operating system. If a large amount of software is to be installed on the system then a large amount of backing storage will be required.

4   (a)

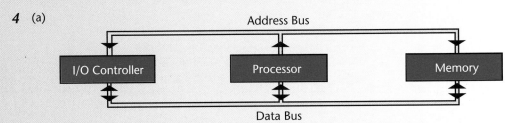

     (b)   Machine code instructions would be transmitted.

          Data would be transmitted such as characters, integers or floating point numbers.

     (c)   0 to 65535

5   (a)

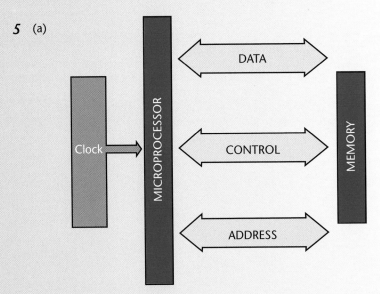

     (b)   The width of the address bus limits the number of addresses that can be accessed and this limits the amount of memory that can be used.

     (c)   A faster clock will allow more operations per second.

          Wider data bus allows more data to be transferred at each store access.

          High speed cache memory can store frequently used data.

          Pipelining can be used to speed up the processing of instructions.

          (Any three of the above will get full marks.)

3 Data representation

1 (a) BA3

(b) The mantissa is 10111010 and the exponent is 0011

As the mantissa is negative we must find the twos complement

	10111010
flip the bits	01000101
add 1	+1
result is	01000110

So the mantissa represents –0.100011.

The exponent is 0011 which represents 3 in denary so we must move the binary point three places to the right giving the value as

–0100.011

Converting the binary number to denary we get

4	2	1	0.5	0.25	0.125
1	0	0	0	1	1
4				+0.25	+0.125 = 4.375

So the value is –4.375

2 (a) (i) 00011110

(ii) 11100010

(b) 10011110

(c) (i) 1D

(ii) Hexadecimal is easy to read whereas the equivalent binary value results in a long string of binary digits that is very difficult to read.

(iii) Each hexadecimal digit represents 4 binary digits. There is no such simple relation between denary and binary.

3 (a) 0000010000000001

(b) 0401

(c) 31303235

4 System software

1 (a) To use the GUI the user clicks on icons to perform tasks.
   To use the CDI the user enters commands at a prompt.
   (b) GUI is easier for novice users as they do not have to remember commands.
   CDI is faster once the commands are known.

2 Operating systems normally provide a hierarchical file structure. The pathname specifies the file's name and also the position of the file in the hierarchy. An example is:

   \WORK\DOCUMENTS\CV.DOC

   \WORK\DOCUMENTS specifies the directory that contains the file
   CV.DOC is the name of the file including the file extension
   .DOC is the file extension that states what type of data will be stored in the file.

3 (a) The user is able to execute a program by using a mouse to move a pointer over its icon and clicking on a mouse button.
   The environment will provide a set of menus that will allow users to select various options.
   (b) It uses more memory than other interfaces.
   It uses more disk space than other interfaces.
   It is slower to operate for an experienced user.

4

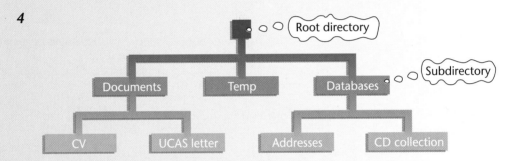

5 (a) A programming language is a set of rules for writing sets of instructions to be run on a computer.
   (b) A low-level language has a one-to-one correspondence with machine code instructions, a high-level language has a one-to-many correspondence with machine code instructions.
   (c) The program needs to be translated into machine code as the computer can only execute machine code programs.

5 Networking

1 (a) The print spooler will store data to be printed until the complete printout is obtained. It allows the user to carry on working while the spooler is printing.

 (b) The user's printer output would be intermingled with other users' output.

2 It is possible to share hardware resources such as printers.
 It is possible to share information that might be of use to several employees.
 It can produce electronic mail (e-mail) to improve communication between employees.

3 (a) Any two sensible suggestions are going to get you the marks. Three examples are given here.
 A company might place information onto the Internet for advertising purposes.
 A company might use the Internet for sales via e-commerce.
 A company might place educational material onto the Internet.

 (b) Again, any two sensible suggestions will get you the marks. Three examples are given.
 Academic research
 Purchasing items via the Internet
 Product research.

4 (i)

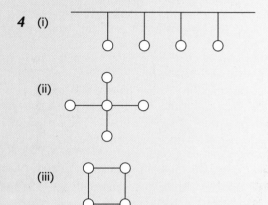

 (ii)

 (iii)

5 Any one advantage from:
 • It provides access to a larger amount of information than will be in the library.
 • It is easier to access than books.
 • It is more fun than using books.
 • It is faster than looking in books.
 • But any other sensible advantage is likely to get the mark.

 A disadvantage may be selected from:
 • Unsuitable material may be found (e.g. propaganda, pornography, etc.).
 • The material may be illegal in this country.
 • Many hours may be wasted looking for material.
 • Material may be factually incorrect.
 • (As above any sensible disadvantage would get you the mark.)

6 Information processing

1 (a) (You must include the first field for identification plus any other three.)
- Employee Number or National Insurance number will be a unique identifier for each employee and will link with the personnel file.
- Tax Code in order to calculate PAYE (income tax).
- Pay to Date – a running total of the employee's pay.
- Tax to Date – a running total of the employee's tax.
- Bank Details so that payment can be made to the employee's bank account.
- Pension Details to enable the deduction of pension payments and eventual calculation of the employee's pension.
- Annual Salary or rate of pay in order to calculate the payment due.

(b) (You must include the first field for identification plus any other three.)
- Employee Number will be a unique identifier for each employee and will link with the payroll file.
- Job Description or Grade to give salary scale and conditions of service.
- Address so that the company can communicate with the employee.
- Department to show where in the company the person is employed.
- Date Joined for calculating length of service.
- Date Left with reason to help with retention of staff.
- Relevant Medical Details to assist with allocating work and/or to help with first aid in case of accident.
- Date of Birth to calculate retirement date.
- Next of Kin in case of emergency.

(c) Payroll would be updated on a regular basis, either once a week or once a month, when everyone's pay is calculated. This would involve a large number of transactions and would be a batch processing task.

Personnel would be updated on an *ad hoc* basis and would be triggered by an unusual event, e.g. promotion, leaving, completion of further qualifications. As this would involve one or two transactions it would probably be done online.

(d) These data would come under the Data Protection Act 1984 so the data should be:
- Collected and processed fairly and lawfully
- Used for the specified registered purposes only
- Relevant and not excessive
- Accurate and up-to-date
- Not kept longer than necessary
- Accessible to the subject for checking purposes
- Security measure must be in place to prevent unauthorised access or alteration of the data.

2 (a) Order Number should be checked by check digit verification or possibly by a range check
Agent Number should also use a check digit.
Date of Order will be validated by a format check and a range check.
Item Number should be checked by check digit verification.
Quantity will have a range check.
Unit Price will also have a range check.

(b) Item ordered is out of stock.
Item number is unused so an invalid item has been ordered.

3 (a) A local area network is a collection of computers connected by cables. It is usually within one building and owned by a single organisation.

(b) A database management system is software that manages a database. It controls access to the data.

(c) Select any three from the following:
- The data will be independent of the application
- The DBMS will maintain data consistency
- There will be less redundancy of data
- Data integrity will be improved
- The data will be more available
- The data can be centrally controlled
- It is easier to keep the data secure.

(d) In order to identify themselves to the DBMS they will need to state an ID (unique identifier) and also a password.

(e) The data should be regularly backed-up and the back-up copies removed to another site or placed in a fireproof safe.

(f) The reference number will act as a unique identifier and it will be used as a key field in the database. It is not possible to use a person's name as there may be more than one patient with the same name.

(g) The practice manager could prepare a budget using the spreadsheet. The budget can then be modified to represent the financial position if different strategies were adopted. The practice manager will be using the spreadsheet package to ask the question 'what if?'.

4

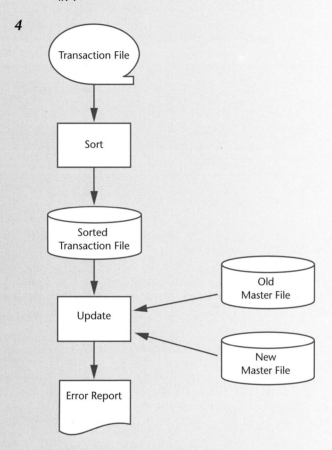

Do not worry if you cannot remember the exact symbols (see Chapter 7). It is more important that you have the correct items and the correct flow lines.

7 Systems development

1

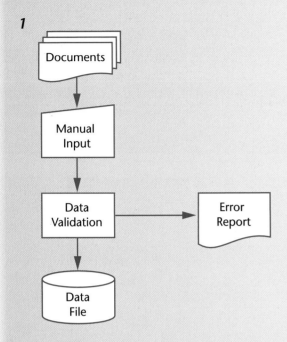

2 (a) Work needed to keep the system operating effectively and fit for the designed purpose, after the system has been implemented.

(b) Perfective maintenance is performed to improve the performance of a system without adding new functions or changing existing functions. An example of perfective maintenance might be to change an algorithm to speed up some process or to change the wording of messages to make them more meaningful.

Adaptive maintenance involves adding or modifying the functionality of the system to reflect the users' requirements. An example might be to add additional reports.

Corrective maintenance is performed to remove bugs that were not found during testing. The type of problems that might be detected are subtle logical errors that only occur under unusual circumstances.

(c) Almost any of the documentation of the system will get you the marks here. You only have to list three.
System flowchart
Algorithms
Properly documented programs
Data models
File structures
Test plans
Original test data and expected results.

3

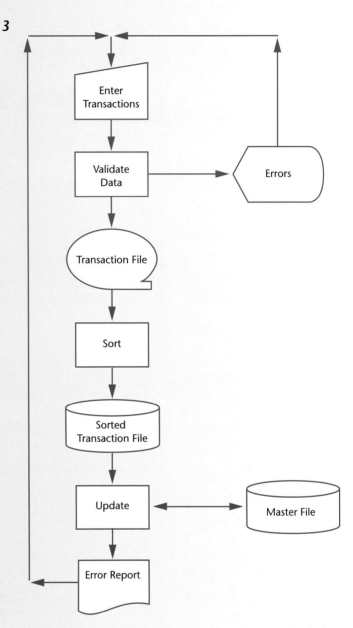

Do not worry if you cannot remember the exact symbols (see chapter 7). It is only important that you have the correct items and the correct flow lines.

8 Programming

1 (a) A high-level language is an English-like problem-solving language, designed for a particular type of problem rather than a particular machine.

    (b) Different languages are designed to solve different types of problems, e.g. FORTRAN or ALGOL (mathematical or scientific problems), COBOL (business problems), C++ (systems programming).

2 (a) Variable with only two possible values, e.g. true/false.

    (b) (i) False

       (ii) True

3 (a)

Low	High	Middle	Found
1	10	5	
6		8	
	7	6	
7		7	True

    (b) This is a search routine. (This routine is actually called a binary search or a binary chop but search is sufficient for the mark.)

Index